DiRTY STOP OUTS GUIDE TO 1970s Liverpool

By Jade Wright

Published by ACM Retro Ltd
www.acmretro.com
A catalogue record for this book is available from the British Library. Other titles in
this series:
Dirty Stop Out's Guide to 1970s Manchester (published November 2017)
Dirty Stop Out's Guide to 1970s Coventry (published November 2017)
Dirty Stop Out's Guide to 1970s Barnsley (published November 2017)
Dirty Stop Out's Guide to 1950s Sheffield.
Dirty Stop Out's Guide to 1960s Sheffield.
Dirty Stop Out's Guide to 1970s Sheffield.
Dirty Stop Out's Guide to 1980s Sheffield.
Dirty Stop Out's Guide to 1990s Sheffield.
Dirty Stop Out's Guide to 1970s Chesterfield.
Dirty Stop Out's Guide to 1980s Chesterfield.
Dirty Stop Out's Guide to 1980s Chesterfield Quizbook.

We're on the look out for writers to cover other UK towns and cities and we're
always on the look out for great retro photos! Please email is at info@dirtystopouts.
com if you fancy getting involved.

www.dirtystopouts.com

DiRTY STOP OUTS GUIDE TO 1970s Liverpool

By Jade Wright

Eric's – short-lived but
a true icon of seventies
nightlife in the city

Contents

Whether Liverpool, Everton or Tranmere, football has always been a big part of Merseyside culture

A Great New Pub with a Grand Old Name

HIGSONS PENNY FARTHING

at the corner of St. Johns Lane,
next to the Royal Court Theatre

 # HIGSONS

INDEPENDENT BREWERS ON MERSEYSIDE SINCE 1780

8

Printed by Codaprint Ltd., 5 Victoria Street,, Liverpool. Tel. 051-236 4802.

Hundreds queue up for a chance of become one of Ken Dodd's Diddymen at the Royal Court Theatre in 1970

Introduction

From the end of Merseybeat to the birth of punk, seventies Liverpool had it all

It was the middle of a decade, but the end of an era.

On June 5, 1973, the rumble of bulldozers and the crashing of masonry echoed up and down Mathew Street as warehouses were torn down and the world-famous Cavern Club filled up with rubble like a grave.

No matter that it was one of the most famous musical venues in the world, no matter that it was the birthplace of the biggest cultural phenomenon of the post-war years, no matter what history had been made there, it was quickly consigned to the past in the name of building a ventilation shaft for the planned underground railway system. A shaft that in the end was never built, the land becoming a storage yard for British Rail vehicles and later a car park – the most mundane monument imaginable to such a magical place.

The demise of the Cavern, where the Beatles had played up to 300 gigs, was just one symbol of the decay blighting Liverpool in the 1970s. The docks,

through which sailors brought the American rhythm and blues records that so transfixed the musicians and DJs of the city, had been declining fast. Seven and a half-miles of that once-great system of floats, piers and cranes closed in 1971, and the last Canadian Pacific Liner shipped out a few years later. Towards the end of the decade, 150,000 could find no work. Liverpool, once a byword for progress and hope, was now a byword for recession and dismay.

While much fell away, the legacy of the music scene of the '60s continued to thrive. The abandoned warehouses that once held corn, grain, sugar and other commodities no longer resounded with the creaking of pulleys and thudding of sacks, but the screeching of electric guitars and the thump of drums. Many of these now cavernous shells became home to the bars and nightclubs that would for many Liverpudlians, living through a bleak decade, be remembered as the places where the most vivid memories were made.

Comedy and cabaret – popular throughout the

9

1960s – continued to thrive, with the golden triangle of Allinson's in Litherland, the Wooky Hollow in West Derby and The Shakespeare in the city centre playing host to some of the biggest comic names. But after the '60s, in which Merseybeat bands had dominated the UK Top 40, Scouse chart hits were relatively few and far between in the '70s.

However, those that did hit the heights continued in the city's trail-blazing tradition as they did so. Liverpool's The Real Thing - started by Chris Amor, Dave Smith, Kenny Davis and Ray Lake in 1970 - topped the singles charts with the super-catchy You To Me Are Everything, becoming the first black British group to have a number one single.

Arty favourites Deaf School were another musical success to emerge, alongside Elvis Costello, who had six top 40 hits in the '70s. While not born in the city, he had grown up in Birkenhead and worked in Merseyside as data entry clerk and computer operator by day, playing gigs across the region at night.

While Liverpool didn't have an arena, large gigs were held either at the Empire Theatre or Liverpool Stadium, which had been built for wrestling but became home to some of the biggest and most memorable concerts of the decade.

Gigs were booked there by Roger Eagle, who the bands loved for his passionate love of music and belief in doing things fairly so musicians got a decent deal. It won him friends across the industry, and set him up well when in 1976 he opened Eric's with fellow music lover and former Deaf School manager Ken Testi. The pair were joined by Peter Fulwell, another fierce champion of grass roots music.

Eric's gave birth to a whole scene, but like all the best clubs, its flame burned bright but briefly. It closed in 1980, but not before cementing its place in Liverpool's popular music history.

North Liverpool was not without its own brilliant clubs, bars and venues. When we started our search for Liverpool's Dirty Stop Outs for this book, we were inundated with stories of granny-grabbing in the Grafton and tropical feasts at the Coconut Grove.

Over the water on the Wirral, there too was to be found a thriving club scene, with dozens of great venues throwing open their doors, and Southport - part of the newly created Borough of Sefton - was another hotbed of activity, with clubs so good they'd draw in crowds from miles around.

Throughout the book we've included as many of your memories and pictures as we can, but we know there are still more stories to tell.

Share your stories and pictures with us at www. facebook.com/liverpoolclubgigmemories - we'd love to see them, and hear about your days as a Dirty Stop Out.

Chapter 1

The end of an era

When he played at Liverpool's 02 Academy a few years ago, Sir Paul McCartney posed an interesting question: "If they can excavate the pyramids, then why not The Cavern?".

For many music fans, the old cellar holds as much history as the oldest of the ancient wonders of the world.

In the early '60s it had been the most important club on the planet, but by the time the '70s came around, The Cavern was struggling.

Owner Alf Geoghegan decided to retire and sold Cavern Enterprises Ltd to Harry Waterman and Roy Adams in September 1970.

It had become a split-level club - with an upper floor of soul music for mods, and the original basement venue for live rock. Wishbone Ash, Nazareth and Stray all played, but as a rule, they were failing to attract the bigger bands and promoters, and had fallen into a vicious cycle. They weren't taking enough on the door to be able to afford to bring in the bigger bands - so then the bigger bands didn't play and they didn't take enough on the door.

Dave Watson used to go in for the rock nights in the early '70s. He remembers: **"It was often quite a confrontational venue because upstairs was a haunt for skinheads who liked blue beats and reggae, then there was also a younger crowd downstairs who wanted to hear rock bands and there was sometimes trouble. At some points they had to serve the drinks in paper cups."**

Rock was a theme for the Cavern in the '70s, including a very early gig from the fledgling band Queen, who played in 1970.

It was the future giant on the city's music scene, Ken Testi, who brought the band to the city.

Ken was living and studying in St Helens at the time.

"My parents had pubs around Merseyside and we moved every few years," he explains. "It was a bit like being on a witness protection program.

"The pub they had in St Helens was next to the college. I was a student there and became social secretary at the students' union."

He was friends with Freddie Bulsara - or Freddie Mercury as the world came to know him - and organised for the new band to come up for a couple of gigs.

"Freddie Bulsara was a friend who had played in a band from Merseyside. When that folded we kept in touch. When he told me that he was forming a band with Brian and Roger I was sure that they would be a good fit and offered to get them a show at the college, as well as to try to get another gig to make the visit more worthwhile.

"They were all Beatles fans and thought that it would be great to work at the Cavern, I warned them that the venue was not the hotspot that it had been, but they were still keen.

"I rang Alf Geogehan, who was the owner at that time. I had placed a few shows there previously for local bands and knew the ropes."

The first gig, in St Helens, was a big success, with the band playing some of their early songs to an appreciative crowd.

"Dressed in their fashionable Kensington market finery Queen cut quite a dash in working class St Helens," laughs Ken. "They stayed at my parents' pub.

"Their musical style and presentation were fully formed from the beginning, and the reception in St Helens was terrific."

When they arrived at The Cavern, they weren't quite as impressed by what they found as they'd imagined they would be.

"The Cavern was almost empty," recalls Ken "But the small audience were appreciative - unlike the scowling DJ upstairs, Billy Butler, for whom, it seemed, a live band were just an inconvenience.

"For me a light turned on, it was my 20th birthday October 30, 1970."

But the lights were fading fast for The Cavern.

In 1972, as British Rail took ownership of the whole section of Mathew Street to build its ventilation shaft, Suzi Quatro became the last major recording artist to perform at the original club, performing in November that year.

Before it was knocked down in the summer of 1973, the famous old red and yellow Cavern sign had been carefully taken down from above the entrance and repositioned on the other side of the street, above the door of 7 Mathew Street, where the new Cavern was opened. It stayed there until 1992, when it was blown down and destroyed during a storm.

As Ken Testi recalls: "The owner of the Cavern when it was compulsorily purchased was Roy Adams. Roy bought premises in the old fruit exchange on the opposite side of Mathew Street and opened them as the New Cavern. But the enterprise failed."

No-one could have foreseen at that time the site was to go on to become something really special later in the '70s.

This is to certify that this is one of 5,000 bricks which Royal Life have salvaged from the original Cavern Club, Mathew Street, Liverpool, England.

Royal Life have sold these bricks, donating the proceeds to a local charity. 1983

H B Johnson. General Manager. Royal Life

R McFall. Founding Owner of the original Cavern Club

Royal Life

Sometimes in more boisterous clubs, the landlords would switch to paper cups

The wives and fiancees of Liverpool FC football players step out in style in the city on a pre-pedestrianised Church Street

End of an Era

LAST NIGHT OF THE OLD

CAVERN

LIVERPOOL'S WORLD-FAMOUS CLUB

SUNDAY, MAY 27, 1973

TICKET £1-25

EMI

SUZI QUATRO

Record Company/Management
RAK RECORDS

Agency : MAM

Suzi Quatro – the last artist to perform at The Cavern

18

The Selecter – champions of the late 1970s 2 Tone movement that was a big hit locally

Chapter 2

The Ropewalks

Fortunately, some things don't change too much. These days The Ropewalks is one of Liverpool's best loved party destinations, and it's easy to see why. The roads around Seel Street, Bold Street, Parr Street, Slater Street and Duke Street have a lively set of mainly independent bars and clubs and attract an eclectic mix of people. In that sense, it hasn't changed much since the '70s, and some of the clubs and pubs have even weathered the test of time.

The Blue Angel

The Blue Angel, or The Raz, as it's affectionately known, is a Liverpool institution that's still going strong.

On the corner, where Seel Street meets Berry Street, The Raz is Scouse club royalty, and has seen more than her fair share of music legends. The Beatles, Rolling Stones and Bob Dylan all played there in the 1960s when it was a jazz club.

Allan Williams was once the owner of the club, and in 1964 reputedly ejected Judy Garland after the local premiere of a film starring a band he used to manage. The band was The Beatles, the film A Hard Day's Night.

It was in the Blue Angel four years before, on August 12, 1960, that Pete Best auditioned to join that up and coming group. It was also where the Beatles, in 1960, auditioned for impresario Larry Parnes, landing them their first tour outside Liverpool, supporting singer Johnny Gentle on a tour of Scotland.

The name 'The Raz' is believed to be named after '60s beauty Rachel 'Raz' Morten, one of George Harrison's early girlfriends.

After seeing Cilla Black performing Bye Bye Blackbird at the Blue Angel, Brian Epstein contracted her as his only female client, on September 6th, 1963.

It's little wonder the building has its own English Heritage Blue Plaque. But it's not there because of any of the musical history, but because in 1805 it was the birthplace of Dr William Henry Duncan, Liverpool's first, and pioneering, Medical Officer of Health.

The club still looks much the same as it did in the '70s, and it's still much loved by University of Liv-

A fight breaks out in the Hofbrauhaus

erpool students, who make it their own on Monday nights. Some say it still has the same carpet. It's certainly sticky enough to have been there even since those heady nights of the early 1960s.

The Cabin Club

Just over the road from The Raz is The Cabin, the club believed to have been the inspiration for The Beatles' song Don't Bother Me. Written by George Harrison while on tour with the band in 1963, the title was said to have come about after the more shy and retiring of the Fab Four's number was harassed by reporters and photographers on his way into the nightclub.

By the '70s it had become a bit of a spit and sawdust club. Literally.

Regular Simon Wilson remembers: "There used to be a layer of sawdust on the floor, and no one was ever sure whether it was just a quirky feature or to disguise the pools of vomit which often appeared later in the night.

"There used to be a huge rocking horse that punters would dare each other to climb onto. There used to be a scary looking fella on the door who wouldn't let you in if he didn't like the look of you.

"Unless, that is, he didn't like the look of you but

thought he could take the mick, and then he'd charge you a tenner to get in.

"Walking into the Cabin is like walking into one of those halls of mirrors at a funfair. You get an odd, surreal feeling in the pit of your stomach. Maybe that's what the sawdust was for."

David Barry Lloyd recalls a woman on the door: "The Cabin Club at the top of Bold Street was run by a certain Mrs Windsor. You were always like 'No, not her!' She wouldn't let you in unless you were wearing a tie.

"You could take if off inside, but if Mrs Windsor was on patrol, you'd be asked to put it back on again. Her logic behind this was to keep the club 'respectable'."

The Babalou

The Babalou on Seel Street was known by many as a friendly club with a mixed clientele. It also hosted gigs, including Judas Priest's September 1972 UK tour.

Former Liverpool bar owner, Russell Start says: "The Babalou was a great place easy to get into. Never any trouble and you could dance all night to great music."

Roger David Smith recalls: "The Babalou was my

favorite. Heavy metal and prog rock on Thursday night. Saturdays were for copping off, if you were lucky. Great times in the seventies.

"I saw a lot of famous bands, before they became well known. TYA, Jethro Tull, Spooky Tooth and lots of others. It was so loud upstairs, downstairs were the bars, and you could cosy up in the cubicles.

"I had very long hair, flares, very loud shirts, boots and a velvet jackets.

"I used to live in Litherland and walked all the way home many times."

The Beachcomber

Dave Jinx Joynson remembers Seel Street favourite The Beachcomber: "Before Eric's opened, the places to be for the alternative crowd to gather was Sundays at La Metro and the fabulous Beachcomber on Thursdays. I went to them both - cannot remember who the DJs were but they did Roxy/Bowie nights that featured Kraftwerk and Deaf School heavily, with loads of sharp dressed people in attendance.

"It was where the robot dance to Bowie's Fame became popular and to the best of my knowledge where The Time Warp was danced to as far back as 1976."

Mike Green also remembers the club with some fondness:

"My favourite poser bar was the Beachcomber [Beachy]. Fairly sophisticated and hard to get a membership card unless you were female. Often

you'd be knocked back on the door depending on the male/female mix inside. Nice laid back atmosphere when you did get in though the women were so far up their own arses you'd rarely tap off. Music was all disco/DJ, and as I recall you could get food there too."

Dulcie Green recalls: "The Beachcomber only admitted members so you had to be in with the in crowd."

The Odd Spot

Arthur Clack had an unfortunate incident in this Bold Street bar and club.

"I only went once," he says. "It was just disco chart stuff with classic slowies. It was your 18-30s and a few older gangsters from what I remember. I was just turned 19 and more interested in my white shirt under the blue fluorescent lights that made it glow purple.

"A new experience for me at the time. It may have put the girls off when they approached and all I said was look at me shirt! It's bright purple!

"Awful old bloke with Brillo hair and gob like a walnut, actually wearing a dirty raincoat and grunting and going 'Oophh!' at all the young women. But even with that for competition, I still didn't cop off."

The Timepiece/Time and Place

Soul and funk were the order of the day at this Fleet Street club, with its colour-changing dance floor. Known as the Time and Place, then The Timepiece,

Early seventies skinheads – a far calmer breed than their counterparts of the early eighties

The Blue Angel, or the Raz, as
she's known to her friends

INTER VIth FORM
Easter Dance
at
"UGLY'S"
50, Duke Street, Liverpool, L
WEDNESDAY, 11th APRIL, 1979.
60p.
8 p.m. to 2 a.m.   NO ADMISSION AFTER 10.30 P.M.
MANAGEMENT RESERVE THE RIGHT TO REFUSE ENTRY

Rockerbilly fashions had a resurgence in the era that saw the death of Elvis Presley

Ugly's of Duke Street

it later became the 147 Snooker Club.

Jen Murray used to work there. She says: "It wasn't that big really. It had a stage and dance floor at one end, a place to get chicken in a basket, and two bars.

"There were booths along one wall and a very bizarre feature - the middle of the room was a sunken seating area, you had to go down six steps to the tables - not easy in high heels after a vino or four!"

DJ Greg Wilson used to travel over from New Brighton to its all-night parties.

"The Timepiece was particularly famed for its all-nighters," he says. "People came from far and wide to attend, in a similar way to what was happening at Wigan Casino, but, of course, with a black audience in the majority."

Greg was playing his own huge nights at the Golden Guinea and the Chelsea Reach by this point, but he always made time to go across the water to The Timepiece.

"It made a huge impression on me and I resolved there and then that this was the type of audience, so knowledgeable with regards to music, that I wanted to play to," he recalls. "Some years later I would

fulfill this aim when I worked with a similar crowd at Legend in Manchester."

He remembers it as one of the few clubs which attracted black music lovers.

"It gave me an insight as to what it must have been like for black people, who were the ones that would usually find themselves, on a day-to-day basis, in the minority and, fairly often, in hostile situations.

"To understand anything about the dance music scene in Liverpool at this time, one huge contemporary myth has got to be exploded, and this involves Northern Soul.

"Northern Soul was not played in every club in the North during this period; in fact it wasn't being played at all in Liverpool. Northern Soul never gained a foothold in Liverpool, where a funkier groove was the order of the day.

"It was also never a factor within the black community in general (be it Liverpool, Manchester or wherever), who weren't interested in digging for rare '60s music when there was a wealth of great funk, soul and reggae released in the '70s."

The Bar Royal

In the early 70s, many of the bars that had provided a safe haven for gay clubbers around Queen Square such as The Magic Clock and the Roebuck had gone to make way for the new St. John's Shopping Centre and bus station.

The Bar Royal on Wood Street was an option for the city's gay community.

23

But there was still some hostility, and guests there were vetted on arrival for safety by owner Sadie. The main door was bolted as people entered. Inside, students mixed with dockers and glamorous members of the trans community mixed harmoniously with lesbians and gay men.

Despite being legalised, homosexuality was still seen as taboo by some, and copies of the Gay Times were still being stocked in brown paper bags at the News From Nowhere bookstore, even into the 1980s.

In time, the scene moved over to Jody's, The Curzon, Lisbon, Paco's, Reflections, Scarlett's and Sadie's, most of which were based on or around Stanley Street in this embryonic stage of what is now the city's Gay Quarter.

Ugly's

Its name wouldn't suggest it would be the home of a beauty contest, but that was Ugly's all over.

The bar and club on Duke Street was popular, particularly on Tuesday nights.

Margaret Reynolds recalls: "Tuesdays were the best."

Colin Evans agrees: "We were never out of there. You had a medallion for a membership card if you were very lucky."

The venue used to hold regular Miss Ugly competitions - where the prettiest girl would win an assortment of prizes, and the questionable accolade Miss Ugly.

Paul Stephens remembers it well: "When I was about 20 I went to Ugly's. There were very steep stairs to the upper disco. I was very naughty in those days and if saw a plain looking girl would say 'did you get in for free?'."

Hollywood

Liverpool hairdresser Herbert Howe opened his own nightclub on Duke Street in the '70s.

His old friend, DJ Pete Price, said of it: "He always said he built it for me to work in. I will never forget the opening night as sadly it was the night my mother died. Herbert was incredibly supportive to me, but Herbert, being Herbert, decided to sack me after the first night, informing me I was too expensive. Only Herbert could get away with that!"

Barbara Kayll remembers Hollywood as "the club that Herbert the hairdryer opened on Duke Street," while Colin Evans adds: "It had very classy decor. Well, you would expect nothing else from the late Herbert."

The Timepiece and its regulars
Photos John Harrison

Enjoying a night out – cabaret style

Chapter 3

London Road, The University and the Georgian Quarter

The area around London Road was booming in the '70s, with great shops and plenty of nightlife too. Wandering from there into the Georgian Quarter, around the university and down into Toxteth there were some great clubs, bars and restaurants.

The Shakespeare

Fondly known as 'The Shakey' this grand old theatre building on Fraser Street saw plenty of drama in the '60s and '70s, with two devastating fires. The first, in November '63, took place just over a fortnight after a £60,000 reconstruction that won it the plaudit of the most elegant nightclub in Britain.

The old Shakespeare Theatre had seen packed houses since 1888, with performances from Sarah Bernhardt and Lily Langtree.

The headline from the front page of that morning's ECHO said it all – Sixty-Minute Blaze Wrecks Luxury Club.

The fire destroyed the roof, gutted the rising stage and damaged the building's galleries, while flames shot 30ft

through the domed roof. A casino within the building was badly damaged by water as more than 70 firemen and 17 fire engines battled the blaze.

The Shakespeare rose phoenix-like from the ashes and became one of the biggest cabaret clubs in Britain, putting on acts including Tommy Cooper, Bob Monkhouse, Bruce Forsyth, Tom Jones and Roy Orbison, with local personality and DJ Pete Price as the compere.

Sheila Wilson remembers nights at the Shakey: "Liverpool was one of the cabaret centres of the country in the '60s, and this continued in the '70s too.

"The finest, till it burnt down, was The Shakespeare in Fraser Street. My mum and dad loved it - and as teenagers we'd get taken as a special treat.

"They'd have a full night's entertainment with a few comedians and groups or comedy groups such as Candlewick Green and Regency Kreme. The night's highlight was always chicken in a basket."

But it wasn't to last. Despite various fire-prevention measures put in after the first blaze, a second inferno took hold and burned it to the ground, and what re-

mained of the structure was demolished.

Sampson & Barlow's/The Peppermint Lounge

Above the restaurant, Sampson & Barlow's on London Road, was a club known in the '70s as the Peppermint Lounge.

In the '60s, it had played host to gigs by Little Richard and, under its previous name The Cassanova Club, saw seven Beatles gigs back in 1961. It had later become a hangout for the Liverpool poets set, with Adrian Henri, Brian Patten and Roger McGough attending its popular folk nights.

As the '70s wore on, it took on more of a disco edge. Sarah Mason remembers it well: "My dad's mate George Blott ran it. I think it used to be called The Cassanova Club and Gullivers and Trophies.

"It had an upstairs function room, and was a great place to go. You'd get wedding receptions in there too. I think there was a restaurant next door called the Yan-Yan, and people would go there after a night out as it never seemed to close."

Joan Kelly adds: "I remember the Peppermint Lounge on London Road, with live bands. The Crying Shames played there."

Pickwick's

Pickwick's was another venue which lots of people remembered very fondly. Kieron Bimpson says: "Pickwicks was great - a massive dance floor with little booths, a huge bar along the back wall. They had cabaret nights and an over 25s disco. Great fun. It was a motley crew of characters - everyone from disco freaks to hen parties, stag dos and everything in between, with cabaret bands and singers during the week too. They built the National Express bus station on the land adjacent."

Hofbrauhaus/Scamps/Studio 1-2-3

A Liverpool Corporation notice in 1969 proclaimed: "Notice is hereby given that the City Council has received an application for planning permission to erect a multi-storey building comprising an entertainments

Kirklands

complex consisting of a Hofbrauhaus, restaurant, three cinemas and a discotheque with two floors of separate offices over, on a site west of the Mount Pleasant multi-storey car park between Brownlow Hill and Mount Pleasant. Included in the proposal is provision for a city walkway. This walkway forms part of a planned system of elevated walkways in the city centre and will connect with a walkway incorporated in the Mount Pleasant car park." Never had a stuffy planning application sounded so exotic.

The proposed walkways didn't happen, but the Scamps, Studio 1-2-3 cinema and the Hofbrauhaus did, bringing with it a Bavarian Oktoberfest style bar to the city, offering steins of beer and lunchtime strippers for the nearby office workers whose productivity no doubt took a slump in the afternoon.

John Campbell recalls: "In about 1978 Hofbrauhaus ran a darts competition with a prize of a small TV for the winner. I entered and in the second round I was drawn to play one of the strippers. There she was in the smallest

pair of knickers - I don't think they had G-strings in those days - and the smallest bra ever.

"It was the best game of darts I've ever played - watching her reach up to take her darts out of the board and bending over to pick them up off the floor when they bounced out - and I'm not just talking about her darts.

"I just about won this game and bought her a drink because it had been a great laugh. I got knocked out of the competition in the next round, but somehow it didn't bother me."

Mardi Gras
The Mardi Gras on Mount Pleasant opened its doors on September 28, 1957. The club's walls were decorated with Beat City murals by Liverpool artist Bob Percival and it was later used for location shots in a Rank film, shot in 1964.

All the top 1960s Liverpool bands played at the Mardi: The Beatles, The Big Three, Gerry and the Pacemakers and Cilla Black, among many others.

By the '70s it was losing its sparkle, but many readers remember it fondly.

Lorraine Goss says: "I remember going fairly regularly to the Mardi Gras - in particular going to the all-nighter when it closed down. I went from 1970 to 1973 and it was pretty run down I guess. I can't be sure but I think Thin Lizzy were one of the bands that played that last night. I'm sure I saw Status Quo play there too."

Originally a church, the building was 225 years old when in 1975 it was demolished to make way for a drab, monolithic concrete car park.

Stars Disco/The Centre Scene
Underneath the hotel building was a club known by various names over the years.

John Martin remembers it as Stars.

"Stars was under The Centre Hotel in Lord Nelson Street, and opened in the early '70s. It was one of the few proper disco clubs in the city, with music coming straight in from New York. It didn't look much, but if you liked music it was a great place to go."

By the late 70s, it was known as The Centre Scene.

Debby Haddley used to go on Sunday nights, where again it was the place to go for a cool, young crowd. "First club I went to was the Centre Scene, around 1977 or 1978," she says. "It was under the Centre Hotel on Lord Nelson Street.

"I went on Sunday nights for their Roxy/ Bowie promotion nights. As well as Roxy Music and Bowie they played English and American punk, and some reggae. Dress code was varied and extreme! There was a good mixture of punk, glam/Bowie, Roxy girls with their pill-box hats. I basically wore anything black."

The unlucky Shakespeare Theatre in its early days

**Mike Rickett
back in his
university days**

The Everyman Bistro
A haven for arty types in the shadow of the Metropolitan Cathedral, the Everyman Bistro is one of the few bars that never lost its cool. Generation after generation of Liverpool students, artists and theatre lovers made their way down the stairs to sample homemade quiche and salads, and hear a word of wisdom from Paddy Byrne and Dave Scott.

Opening in the summer of 1970, the Bistro was a landmark, and served great food at relatively low prices. In the days when pubs had to close by law at 10.30pm, the only way to get a late drink was to buy a meal as well, and there were few better places to do it than the Everyman.

In the early '70s, patrons were marshalled through the theatre foyer by big-hearted doorman Les Hancock, before the rebuild of the late '70s saw the Bistro got its own front door and an extra room.

Those were the days when you'd be eating and drinking next to the actors. Pete Postlethwaite, Julie Walters, Bill Nighy, Jonathan Pryce, Trevor Eve, Bernard Hill, Anthony Sher and Barbara Dickson were all regulars on stage and off.

In the late '80s a third room was opened to meet demand and recently the theatre was completely renovated, including stripping the old Bistro back. During the building works, Paddy opened up The Pen Factory, a few doors down Hope Street, where he remains.

University Life
Liverpool's university and polytechnic brought the young and trendy to the city. From the university's position at the top of the hill, close to the city's two cathedrals, it attracted a cool group of kids to what's now called the Georgian Quarter, but what is really Toxteth, or L8 as it's often known.

They were eager to enjoy everything the city had to offer.

Mike Rickett came to Liverpool in 1970 and remembers those days well.

"I can't quite remember where the party started. It could well have been the Cas – as it was known – or to give it its proper name the Casablanca on Hope Street. It was a favourite venue for misfits, eccentrics, criminals and the more adventurous students like me.

"So, the party at the Cas developed along traditional lines of booze, whacky chats with pseudo intellectuals, dancing and attempting to make my number with the girls.

"I was in my first year of an English degree at Liverpool University and according to my lecturers I was unlikely to graduate to the second year unless I actually began to do a little work. Not unreasonable, I suppose, but I was intoxicated by my new exciting world of crazy people doing crazy things. Work could come later."

Like many students who'd come to the city in the 70s, he was initially attracted by the music and fell in love with the creative scene he found.

"It was 1970 and Liverpool was THE place to be," he says. "Music was everywhere, girls were everywhere. It was a good time to be a student and Liverpool was a magnet for people from all over the UK.

"Added to that was the substantial achievement in getting to university at a time when only something like 5% of kids went on to higher education. And like many others I was the first in my family to achieve this."

As well as high spirits, there were other substances floating around campus at that point too.

"I can't quite remember why I started to experiment with acid," says Mike. "At the time, it just seemed the thing to do, especially at parties, and there was always a party to go to.

"The very first time it just blew my mind and I could understand why Lennon wrote some of his songs. The colours, the sounds, the feeling that you could wrap your consciousness around the universe.

"True, it did have its downsides. There were many reports in the papers at the time of kids jumping off buildings thinking they could fly. Fortunately, I was not one of them.

"I would be on a different planet for a few hours communing with all my gods!

"On this occasion though the trip was different. Very, very different. Gone were the psychedelic colours, gone was the feeling of euphoria, gone was communing with the gods. Instead there was a deep voice telling me that my life was over and that I should end it; everywhere was black or purple and I was rigid with terror. But worse was to come. Much, much worse.

"I was, apparently, screaming and people were slapping me and pouring water over me and the next thing I knew I was in my bed with a headache the likes of which I had never had before.

"That was my last trip. Ever."

How about the degree?

"Believe it or not I did graduate," he says. "And with a 2:1. My professor could not believe it. And neither could I."

Buzzcocks / Joy Division: Tuesday 2 October 1979, Mountford Hall, Liverpool, by Dave Wiggins

Strange as it may seem, it all started in North Wales. Like many Scouse teens, I undertook the rite of passage that was 'working the season'. Lots went to Rhyl, but I opted to travel slightly further along what is now the A55, and chose to find gainful summer employment in the rather more genteel resort of Llandudno.

Like most people who watched television in the 1970s, I had seen the Sex Pistols being set up by Bill Grundy, and was rather amused by the subsequent 'The Filth and the Fury' faux outrage. At 15, I was too young to go to the legendary 'Eric's' club, in Mathew Street, but soon got into a number of the Punk / New Wave acts that sprung up in 1977/78. My leanings, though, were largely chart based (The Jam, for example), and I didn't have any substantive gigging experience to speak of.

Upon arrival at The Ritz, in Mostyn Street, I was paired up with Michael, who, today, would probably be called my 'mentor'. He was local and had worked the previous season, so knew the drill. His spiky hair and a small 'Clash' badge on his waiter's shirt suggested that this was someone that I would get on with. And so it proved. He started taking me to the Thursday night disco, at the County Hotel, where the DJ would compartmentalise his music into 20 minute chunks – chart hits of the day ('Ring my Bell', 'Lost in Music', 'Ain't no stoppin' us now); 'grebo' (Status Quo, Rainbow, AC/DC); and then a New Wave section for the under-represented pseudo punx.

It was the latter that grabbed me; in particular, I was blown away by Stiff Little Fingers' 'Alternative Ulster', which remains one of my favourite all-time singles to this very day. I returned to our Kensington (Liverpool version) maisonette, in September 1979, an authentic Punk Rocker (albeit two years too late), and vowing to get out to real live gigs. I was true to my word; over the next 8 weeks, I saw The Boomtown Rats, Siouxsie and the Banshees and The Jam (the latter at Deeside Leisure

Centre, where utter carnage would ensue, and which needs an article in its own right).

I was also seduced into town on a wet Tuesday night, to see Buzzcocks. Riding high in the charts with the paean to unrequited love 'Ever fallen in love (with someone you shouldn't've)', they had invited fellow Mancunians, Joy Division, to open for them on this tour. This turned out to be a grave mistake, as history records that – to coin a phrase – Joy Division blew the headline act off stage. I was transfixed by Ian Curtis, as he flailed around the stage; eyes staring at everything and, then, nothing (his health issues were not widely known, at that time). They were incredible, and I can here confirm what many previously thought to be an urban myth. Dozens of punters did depart following Joy Division's set; knowing that nothing could hope to follow that.

I didn't. I stayed for Buzzcocks, and really enjoyed them. My thoughts on the walk home, though, were all about the support band. Building up the courage to go into 'Probe', and face the terrifying Pete Burns, I purchased 'Unknown Pleasures' the very next day. I played it ceaselessly, for months, whilst awaiting the release of the follow-up. Only 7 months after the show, though, Joy Division were no more. Beset by health and personal problems, which he felt were insurmountable, Ian Curtis chose to take his own life. The album, Closer', released in the summer of 1980, was a thing of beauty and a fitting tribute. Indeed, his own lyrics – when examined with hindsight – foretold how this particular tragedy might play out.

Typing this nearly 38 years after that legendary gig, the memories are flooding back. And an apposite Ian Curtis line seems the only way to conclude my short tale: "If you could just see the beauty; things I could never describe".

Chauffeurs'
Now home to restaurant 60 Hope Street, Chauffeurs' was opened in an old house as an upmarket club for the city's well-heeled.

Jason Raw remembers trying to get into Chauffeurs'. "Everyone used to say you had to know someone to get in," he says. "The door staff were very tough, and given that it was in an old Victorian house I used to feel like a little street urchin trying to get through the door.

"One night it was snowing and they finally let me in. I thought they'd taken pity on me, but looking back I suspect they weren't overwhelmed with customers that night - no-one with any sense would have gone out.

"I remember it was like an old gentleman's club inside, very grand, with leather armchairs and big roaring fires. I felt a bit out of place, and I never went back. Give me Eric's any day!"

Rumblin' Tum/The Sink
Rumblin' Tum, with its basement Sink Club, was one of the city's first black music venues when it opened back in 1958. It got its name because entry was by way of a numbered sink plug on a short length of chain which proved membership.

Now known as the Magnet, the legendary basement club is still going, as one of the few remaining original venues in the country.

Over the years it's played host to acts including Ibis, Gregory Isaacs, Ron Ayers, Deaf School and Pete Wylie. Freddie Mercury and Brian May played there with their band Smile, an early incarnation of what later became Queen.

It's had a variety of guises, including a Las Vegas style gambling hall, but is best known for its original Sink playlist of '60s soul and Motown, rhythm and blues and Jamaican sounds, played by Stan Evans, Pete Everett, Dennis Haw and Tony Brookes. It still hosts gigs from those DJs on some Sunday afternoons.

Kirkland's
Kirkland's cafe bar opened in 1976, a sophisticated continental wine bar with chairs and tables out on the pavement. The building was a bakery until the 1970s, known as Kirkland Jennings, with royal appointment crest.

Under the watchful eye of Bernie Start, Kirkland's was both a daytime cafe culture venue, and a cool bar late into the night. It eventually closed in 1999, and has since re-opened as the Fly in the Loaf.

Chaucer's
Across the Hardman Street was another cool bar with musical connections, Chaucer's. Well known for its live gigs from bands such as Deaf School, it was well loved by the arty student set.

O'Connor's Tavern
Another key venue in the city's music history was O'Connor's Tavern, which had played host to poets Roger McGough and Adrian Henri, as well as Mike McCartney in his Scaffold days.

Ken Testi remembers meeting a particularly significant band there in the '70s: "I played bass guitar in a Liverpool band called Great Day. It wasn't working out and we decided to play our last gig at O'Connor's Tavern on Hardman Street.

"Fledgling art school band Deaf School asked if they could play a support slot. It was their first public show. They brought many from the college and the place was packed. The number in the band was well into double figures with instruments as diverse as euphonium, violin and banjo alongside the more conventional.

"Not yet accomplished musicians, they relied on the quality and presentation of their ideas to wow the crowd. Audacious and enigmatic, seasoned musicians present dismissed them as no-hopers, but for me a light turned on. I became their tour manager. It was early in 1974."

Mardi Gras

Thanks to John Harrison for this picture of Chauffeur's

Debby Haddley at the Centre Scene

Dave Wiggins and friends

Q Tips – fronted by
Paul Young who found
massive solo success
in the early 1980s

Chapter 4

Lime Street and the
heart of the city

The heart of the city saw some big changes in the '60s, '70s and early '80s, owing largely to the building of St John's Shopping Centre, which opened in 1969, with St John's Market unveiled to the public by Queen Elizabeth II in April 1971.

This was before the Clayton Square redevelopment, and in the days when the old Prince of Wales News and Gala Theatre still stood. By this point it was long past its best, and known as the Jacey Film Theatre, showing mostly adult movies.

This was in the days when Cases Street went straight through to the square, with its pubs The Sefton, Casey's and the Egerton Arms. The historic square was demolished in 1986 to make way for another shopping centre.

The Top Rank Suite, Bailey's, Romeo and Juliet's, Studio 54 and Rotters

The biggest destination was probably the Top Rank Suite, which was perched on the top of the St John's Centre.

Top Rank was a chain of nightclubs across the country owned by the Rank Organisation. **They were often known as Top Rank Suites or Top Rank Ballrooms. They were immortalised in two '70s songs - Althea & Donna's 1977 number one Uptown Top Ranking, and The Moody Blues track Top Rank Suite, on their 1978 album Octave.**

Over the years, this site was known as The Top Rank Suite, Romeo and Juliet's, Bailey's, Studio 54 and Rotters.

Jen Murray remembers it well: "The Top Rank was absolutely massive. There was a stage, shiny dance floor in front of that and then loads of tables and chairs. A really long bar along one side, so the boys could eye up the girls at the tables!

"Then it had an upstairs, where you could look down and people watch, and another long bar of course. They had some well-known people perform there."

John Glass says: "I stayed off school to go to the

Top Rank's opening. Radio 1 Roadshow. Think it was July 1968 but it was a long time ago so I may be wrong."

Barbara Kayll went to see a well-known act - and ended up seeing two.

"I went to see 10cc at the Top Rank. Tickets were 50p and believe it or not their support band were Queen!" she says. "But I only remember having eyes for the drummer in 10cc. It was in the early '70s. Strangely enough, my husband of 33 years was there as well, but we didn't know each other. We met later in a wine bar called Plummers in Hardman Street in the early '80s."

Jeanette Hough was also a regular. "What I can remember about the Top Rank was that it had a big balcony that overlooked the dance floor, and my future father-in-law heard a rumour that my husband had fallen off the balcony."

Sheila Burns remembers her mum working there. "She was a cleaner and used to take me to the Saturday morning disco, I think around 1970. I had my first slow dance there and I was shaking like a leaf."

Carolyn Wignall Drake also worked at the Top Rank. She says: "Trying to earn some extra money me and my friend Sue Everall got a second job working at the Top Rank. A bonus of course was being able to see some great and legendary bands. The night David Bowie performed was absolutely amazing. I 'collected glasses 'all night."

Peter Creaby was also there for that gig. "The Top Rank - they had a revolving stage if my memory serves right. My claim to fame is I saw Dave Bowie there.

"He had just made Ziggy Stardust. In those days in football Martin Peters was supposed to be ahead of his time. Well Bowie obviously was in the music arena.

"We were into soul, James Brown, etc. My elder brother played The Beatles and Dusty Springfield non-stop so we jumped into the new soul era straight away with Tamla Motown.

"Bowie was dressed like he was from another planet and his music was to us. Now obviously we know we had witnessed something special that night. We paid our 50p on the door and Bowie came on stage at 10pm. The date was September 4, 1972. I was nineteen at the time."

Not everyone enjoyed the acts so much. Valerie Jones recalls: "I remember Ken Goodwin dying a death there. Every time he told a joke, the audience gave the punchline. It was awful."

Like many of the others around the country, the Top Rank Suite changed its name to Bailey's, although they still had a focus on live music.

Bryony Holden remembers going to Bailey's.

"At 13 years old in 1973, I had my make-up and hair done, and wore my sister's blue maxi skirt, and a turquoise sparkly halter top to get into a gig my brother was playing. Sitting with mum and dad, sipping my lemonade trying to blend in, feeling a million dollars. A guy comes up and asks me to dance. And I said 'Dunno. I'll have to ask my dad.'"

Steve Hesketh says: "I think it would have been 1973 when I started going. I went every weekend around 1974 and 1975, and saw Mud, Showaddywaddy, the New Seekers, The Stylistics, Billy Ocean, The Chi-Lites, The Rubettes and Roxy Music. It was the background to my best years - great times.

"I had the Elton John shoes - brown and beige platforms with the big star on - they killed me!

"Thankfully no pictures from those days. It was a different era. I didn't have a house or car or any worries."

John Jones is also glad of a lack of photographic evidence. "I always wore a three piece and a pair of

cream platforms. I'm so glad there are no pictures!"

Jean Pritchard also saw Showaddywaddy at Baileys. "They were good live," she says. "Then either on Christmas Eve or Christmas night The Real Thing were on. You had to get tickets for this. Can you imagine bands of today playing over Christmas? Wouldn't happen. I think this was in 1974.

"Liverpool used to get some big stars before the age of arenas. I have seen Slade, Diana Ross, Elton John, Eric Clapton on the Empire. Also the stadium had good bands and wrestling. Saw Osibisa on a cold winter's night. They were immense."

With another year it was another name change. Bobby Owens worked at Romeo and Juliet's after it changed its name from Bailey's. "I worked their when it was Romeo and Juliet's with my mate John Waters," he says. "I think it was about 1976 or 1977. Loved it. There were two levels, two dance floors, large ballroom and stage. Five bars. Lots of live bands.

"I started as a glass collector then when Alfie the cellar man broke his hand punching a wall at a party I got his job for a bit."

After a stint as Studio 54, its final guise was Rotters, which it remained until the '80s. Debby Haddley recalls: "I still have my membership card with the wrong date of birth on it. I'd added a couple of years so I could get in!"

John Mcilwaine from Manchester remembers Rotters well: "The DJ John Barry left Manchester and went to Liverpool. We all went to see him and he set up a dancing competition between Rotters Manchester regulars and Liverpool regulars - six people from each club took part, they emptied the dance floor and played three songs, the crowd would decide who was best by loudest cheer. We clearly won but John was worried there would be a riot so declared a draw and we all got bottles of champagne! They were really friendly there."

The Moonstone
Part of the same '60s block as the Top Rank Suite, the Moonstone had been a popular hangout for the hippy movement. Hippies were something of a minority within the city's subcultures, but the Moonstone catered for a more alternative crowd like them. They were known as 'troggs' locally.

It was a friendly venue, when many weren't quite so open to other tribes or subcultures. Not since the days of trad jazz had there been such strong divisions in pop music that ran along precise lines of dress, lifestyle and even social class.

Several local bands played at the Moonstone, but the major group for many of these 'troggs' were Restless. Invariably when Restless appeared, the venue was packed. Following the end of an evening's sessions, 'troggs' would often move onto the Cavern, the Stadium, or perhaps the Mardi Gras.

The Penny Farthing
Paul Stephens was also a big fan of live music. He remembers: "Top Rank had top artists on every month. We met up in the Penny Farthing upstairs, sitting on the revolving couch. Great fun with strangers one minute looking at St. George's Hall, next facing Rose-Ann the barmaid. The look on their faces was enough to make us fall into fits of laughter."

The Star and Garter
Carol Meacock says: "A lot of people don't mention some of the fab pubs where the groups would play. The Star and Garter to see Liverpool Express every Tuesday, The Masonic all the Soul groups and the Sportsman. My friend and I are on the poster outside the Cavern pub celebrating 50 years of the Cavern."

Late seventies punk idol Siouxsie

A lively night at the Hofbrauhaus

Posing outside the Top Rank in 1974

Top Rank Suite
Photo: John Harrison

**The Moonstone,
St Johns Precinct**
Photo: John Harrison

Rotters
Photo: John Mcilwaine

Cases Street
Photo: John Harrison

Richard Cummins building
St John's Beacon
Photo: Gary Cummins

Chapter 5

St John's Beacon
- the 'chippy on a stick'

With its vantage point across the city and views over to Wales on one side and the Pennines on the other, St John's Beacon was the place to be when it opened in 1969.

It housed a viewing deck and a revolving restaurant, known fondly as 'the chippy on a stick'. But this was a fancy menu - if there were chips, they'd be frites, as the initial menus were entirely in French.

Jean Pritchard was one of the lucky diners. She says: **"Some friends went and the man chose steak tartare, not realising it was raw!"**

Thankfully Jean had a better time when she visited. "It was winter and as we were having our dinner it started snowing," she says. "It was fantastic seeing the rooftops and the city turn white.

"It was expensive though, compared to the rest of the city's restaurants, but a great experience to see the city from a different aspect and a good place for a special occasion. Pity we didn't have camera phones in those days."

While the revolving restaurant was great for seeing the view, it wasn't without its issues, as DJ Billy Butler explains: "The difficulty was when you went to the toilet your table wasn't in the same place when you came out."

Debbie Maloney had a similar problem: "I went with a boyfriend. He had just inherited his grandma's cash and wanted to impress me. It was during the week and so was very quiet up there.

"We had champagne and a fabulous steak dinner. Fantastic view of the Mersey and beyond, and the sunset was amazing.

"It would have been a brilliant experience, but for two things. First I was so squiffy that when I came back from the loo, I sat down at the wrong table with total strangers, as the restaurant had revolved and I hadn't realised.

"The second was for days I was ill, not with the food but with motion sickness. Never saw him again after that."

Georgina Wilson was also wined and dined on a date, with similar consequences. "A new boyfriend

39

**Hi-rise sophistication –
dining at the revolving**

took me there in 1974, and then I had to chip in as he couldn't afford the whole bill.

"The revolving scene made me a bit giddy, but it was spectacular. I kept my meal down in the restaurant, but nearly gave it them back on the way down as the lift dropped like a stone and I had legs like noodles trying to walk out."

Dulcie Green also suffered with the motion of the revolving restaurant. "I must have been about six. I think we went with my mum's rich boyfriend because it was the place to be seen at the time.

"I had lobster. I think I was sick as well, because it didn't go that slowly from what I can remember."

Ray Nash was one of the lads who took his girlfriend up the tower to impress her. "I got engaged in that restaurant. My biggest memory is the cost. I didn't know it was a la carte and just had enough for the meal. Mr Romance had to ask his new fiancée if she had any change for the bus. She cried."

Kenneth Speed was another diner shocked at the cost of the menu. "Peas at ten bob a portion! A lot of money then."

Sandra Chapman Ford remembers it fondly. "My sister came over from America about 1970 with her husband. They came over on the QE2 or whatever it was then. They had their Cadillac shipped over too. They took us all there for a meal.

"There were 10 of us altogether. We all piled in the Cadillac and were very posh going into town. The bees' knees!

"My brother in law ordered pate and was disappointed. It was tinned it just looked like spam.

"My sister and brother-in-law had a restaurant in US. My brother, who was about 11, asked for frogs' legs. The waiter came back saying they didn't have any. l told him they must have hopped off.

"It was lovely seeing the city from above especially at sunset. My brother in law got a bit dizzy too. Not used to the beer as well."

Andrew Clarke took his in-laws for dinner there in his new car. "I took my wife and father-in-law there for a night out. He panicked when he looked down and couldn't see my lovely new Citroen CX parked below.

"He'd forgotten that we were slowly turning."

Sandra Carter was another diner who struggled with the revolving restaurant when she visited for her anniversary. "We had our twelfth anniversary meal there. I had a job finding our table on returning."

Debbie Challinor has fond memories of meals there with her mother. "Mum took us there a few times when we went to town shopping. It was a real treat. I loved sitting having dinner while tower revolved seeing every point of Liverpool and beyond. So magical."

Gary Cummins has a family connection to the tower. "My uncle Richard Cummins was the Foreman crane operator for it. He finished building it in 1969."

David Wall was a member of the team. He says: "I used to be a chef there. The menu was very good at the time. Before I left I was on the sauce section, making veloutes, demi glass, provencale, lobster bisque. It was always busy. One of my favourites was château-briands - a double fillet steak, bouquet of vegetables and served with a bearnaise sauce.

"Oh, and profiteroles smothered in Cadbury's chocolate sauce with fresh whipped cream, garnished with shards of dark chocolate.

"I remember a lot of the staff. The manager was Mr Angel Izuel, the chefs were Ian Cobham, John Malpelli, Derek Hughes, Dave Hardran, Jimmy Spears. There was John the lift man, and Ken Smith. It was owned by United Biscuits.

"It was long hours. I used to finish at 10.30pm and go straight to Tiffany's nightclub."

Lynne Amena remembers being served by Angel Izuel. "I dined in there a few times in 1971. I still have a certificate to say I dined in orbit. The maître d' was called Angel - very appropriate."

Bernie Cooke was impressed by the view. "I was

Richard Cummins building St John's Beacon
Photo: Gary Cummins

there when the oil rig was launched from Birkenhead. It took about an hour to rotate 360 degrees. What a view!

"A guy called Colin Bentley wanted to turn it into a Star Wars experience with lasers that children could control. Me and a friend looked at doing the work but I think the airport put an end to the plans."

Not everyone was as fond of heights.

Poor Colette Molloy was petrified when she visited. "I was 17 so in 1974 or '75. I worked for Tilney and Company stockbrokers in Exchange Flags. All the staff were paid for to go for our staff Christmas dinner. I'm terrified of lifts and heights but I had no choice!"

Barbara Kayll was another nervous diner. "I went up there when I worked at the Playhouse Theatre in the late '70s. I was dared to go on the viewing deck! I was terrified and clung to the wall - a horrible experience!

The restaurant, viewing platform, and a later cafe, were popular with children too.

Janet Thurling says: "We took the kids up the tower but not into the restaurant. The high-speed lift was amazing, as was the view."

Fran Jones adds: "I took my sons there for a birthday party. Most tables were by the windows so if you looked up you could be looking at the Wirral and the next time in land over the city. Night time it was posh but daytime not so much. I took a group of five to seven-year-olds. Their taste then was more sarnies and trifles!"

The original restaurant closed in 1979 over health and safety concerns. It was re-opened, with a reduced capacity and additional fire prevention measures, and eventually re-fitted as a Buck Rogers space-themed restaurant.

Peter Nicholson remembers: "I remember there being a cafe at the top - not the restaurant - selling tea coffee and biscuits, and putting 2p in viewing binoculars, of which you could see some great views around the city."

The cafe closed due to lack of business. After this the observation deck and the restaurant remained shut for years and the tower lay empty. Often dubbed a white elephant, it had blue go faster stripes added in 1994, later removed upon refurbishment.

The tower was refurbished in 1999 at a cost of £5 million. It reopened as Radio City 96.7 (and Magic 1548) in August 2000. The outdoor observation deck which had been located on the roof of the restaurant was transformed into a second floor. This now holds offices and conference rooms for the radio station. The studios are on the lower floor that used to be the restaurant.

Once again the public can go up and see the city from a viewing gallery, although it no longer revolves. The original revolving structure and machinery were left intact during the refurbishment, but brackets were added to lock the moving structure in place.

PINK FLOYD
TOUR '72

Jan.	20th	The Dome, Brighton
	21st	Guildhall, Portsmouth
	22nd	Winter Gardens, Bournemouth
	23rd	Guildhall, Southampton
	27th	City Hall, Newcastle
	28th	Town Hall, Leeds
Feb.	5th	Colston Hall, Bristol
	10th	De Montfort Hall, Leicester
	11th	Free Trade Hall, Manchester
	12th	City Hall, Sheffield
	13th	Empire, Liverpool

FEBRUARY 17th, 18th & 19th
RAINBOW THEATRE, LONDON

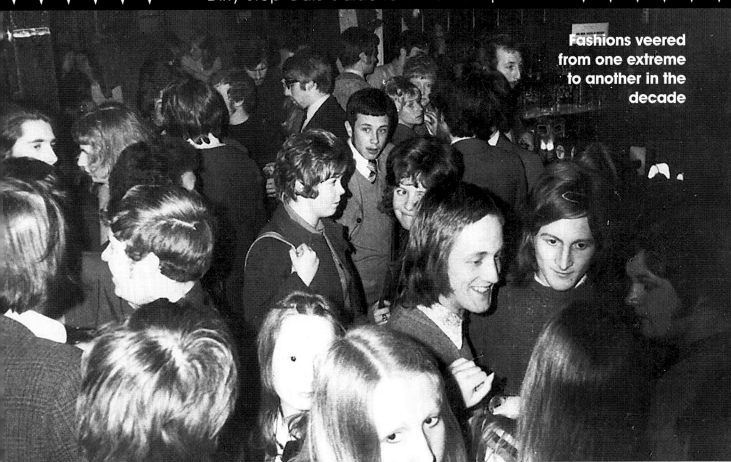

Fashions veered from one extreme to another in the decade

Chapter 6
The Empire Theatre

When we think of Liverpool's great gig venues, it's easy to miss out The Empire. The grand old theatre welcoming visitors to the city from Lime Street Station next door is more of a traditional panto and musicals venue these days.

But in the '60s and '70s it was a well-known gig venue on the circuit, playing host to some of the biggest gigs of its age.

After gigs from The Beatles, Roy Orbison, The Who, Jimi Hendrix and Pink Floyd in the '60s, joining the likes of Bing Crosby, Frank Sinatra and many other internationally known stars.

By the time the '70s came around it was on a roll, with two Royal Command performances for the Queen and Prince Charles and a gig list that read like a who's who of '70s chart acts.

"The Empire was a great place to see a live band," says John Reid from Tuebrook. "I remember one of the first shows I ever saw there was the Rolling Stones in March 1971. They did two shows that day. I saw the first. I have no idea how they had enough energy to do both. I was exhausted just watching.

They kicked off with Brown Sugar, then Jumpin' Jack Flash and Sympathy For the Devil. They played Let It Bleed, Honky Tonk Woman and Street Fighting Man. I remember it like it was yesterday.

"They were so full of energy and swagger. I was mesmerised.

"I only wish I'd kept my ticket. You handed them in on the door, but I'd have loved it as a memento."

David Bowie played two sold-out shows at the Empire on June 10, 1973. He'd arrived at the Empire wearing blue trousers and a silver jacket, surprising fans with his bright orange hair. The star was recently back from a tour across America and Japan. The show itself began with music from a Clockwork Orange before launching into a set of hits.

Backstage with Paul McCartney at the Liverpool Empire, by William Leece former Liverpool Echo reporter

The 1970s may have been the know-it-all decade after the joyous psychedelic innocence of the 1960s, the decade of a brave new world that started with flights to the moon being almost commonplace, but it was

William Leece (centre) and friends

also a time when life was somewhat simpler.

The PR industry was gathering momentum, to be sure, but the over-protective and manipulative spin doctors of later years had yet to materialise. Brazen effrontery could get you a long way as a reporter, and if that failed there was always low cunning.

So it was that in 1973 a deputation of Liverpool hacks and snappers assembled at the stage door of the Liverpool Empire. Paul McCartney was in town for his first gig since the Beatles' touring heyday in the mid-60s - but he'd forgotten to pencil in a chat with the Echo.

The jobsworth guarding the door wanted to keep it that way. 'No, sorry, you can't come in,' he declared. No, he wouldn't phone and ask.

Someone tried the direct approach. 'We know where the green room is, it's just up there,' and in he marched. The rest of the Liverpool press corps followed, and the voice of the jobsworth followed us up the stairs. 'He's not giving interviews, he's on stage in an hour, you can't go there...' The final protests were lost in the echoes.

I can't remember now whether we knocked, or just marched straight in. Paul was there with Linda, and they didn't seem at all put out. Sit where you like, we were told, and fire away with the questions.

As the youngest member of the crew I was a bit overawed by it all, and let the senior reporters lead the way. But when Paul asked, 'Has anyone got a Number 6', I was the first to reach into my pockets and produce a packet of ciggies. We both lit up, and it was then that Steve Shakeshaft took a picture of Paul

with the Number 6 I'd just given him, which has been reprinted over and over again in the Echo and many other publications.

Eventually, he called the meeting to a halt. 'I'm gonna have to ask you to go now, we're on stage in a few minutes.' And that was it. Everyone was given a souvenir Frisbee branded with the Red Rose Speedway album Paul and Wings had just released, and Linda handed an enormous bouquet of flowers - presented by the Empire - to a flabbergasted Margaret Hyde – then a young BBC Radio Merseyside reporter.

There was one final twist to the tale. At the bottom of the steps, a slightly flustered roadie intercepted us and warned Paul 'George Harrison's in the building somewhere'.

He was, frankly, panicking a bit. Then from along a corridor appeared the avuncular figure of George himself. No, not the ex-Beatle, but the former Echo feature writer who'd covered the Fab Four from the earliest days.

They were both genuinely delighted to see each other. 'Hello George, how're you doing?' and 'Paul, good to see you,' and so on.

Of all the memories of that night, none sticks in my mind better that the utter bewilderment on the part of the roadie as he was introduced to the other George Harrison.

Two final points. Paul and I have both long given up cigarettes. And the baccy was not wacky.

The following year saw more great gigs - including Electric Light Orchestra and Emerson, Lake &

**Ian Prowse (centre)
and in later years**

Palmer in March, Black Sabbath in May, Wishbone Ash in October and a double bill of Golden Earring and Lynyrd Skynyrd in November. Possibly the venue's biggest gig of was Pink Floyd, who played the Empire Theatre on November 14.

Another huge year for gigs was 1976, which saw shows from Rick Wakeman, the return of Electric Light Orchestra, a set from Aerosmith, Barclay James Harvest and more from Wishbone Ash.

Bryan Ferry at the Liverpool Empire 27/2/1977 by Dave King

The Liverpool Empire in 1977 was Liverpool's main concert venue, located just beside Lime St Station and holding a capacity crowd of around 2350 people. It was a real plush affair with red carpets and even a Royal box and it catered for everything from the opera to rock concerts.

Tonight's turn was none other than the king of cool himself Mr Bryan Ferry. Together with his band Roxy Music he and David Bowie trail blazed their brands of glam/art rock music through the early '70s all over the UK.

In 1977 he decided to go for a full international solo tour moving slightly away from Roxy Music towards a retro soul sound. He was at the top of his game in 1977 with sell out tours and huge album sales as well as dating the model Jerry Hall. But a change was in the wind for Mr Ferry and his like as punk was about to explode onto the streets of Britain and Jerry Hall was to have her head turned by Mick Jagger in late 1977.

Nevertheless this was his night and it was a sold-out gig for Mr Ferry and his band of Roxy members and hired guns such as Chris Spedding on guitar and a full brass section. A Roxy/Ferry audience was a sight to behold in 1977.

No scruffy double denim jeans and jackets here. The men wore cool suits or white tuxedos with black tie and the women wore fake fur wrap-arounds, cocktail dresses and stiletto heels made off with '40s era hairstyles. Style was in abundance and when Bryan walked onstage the girls swooned and I witnessed a girl at the front throw her garter at Bryan which landed on his shoulder and cool as you like he brushed it aside!

Bryan had an album to promote named In Your Mind and he played songs from this as well as his previous solo hits and a good measure of cover versions such as the Everly Brothers The Price of Love. Although he had Roxy members onstage - such as Paul Thompson on drums and Phil Manzanera on guitar - he stayed clear of any Roxy Music songs proving that his solo career was proving as successful as his band career.

The next day as I was still only 15 years old I had to get up and take the boring bus journey to my now long gone Roman Catholic high school in downtown Birkenhead. I would be leaving school this year and as I climbed the stairs to the cigarette filled top floor of the bus I could see the dark looming sight of the Cammel Laird Ship yard in the distance and the very real prospect of ending up there that year terrified me. Thankfully I managed to escape its future grip.

It was a grey world I lived in in 1977 but on that morning I closed my eyes and my world was lit up with colour as I was the boy with Roxy in his head.

In 1977 its owners Moss Empires reviewed plans to dispose of the theatre after making a loss over the previous five years, and two years later in April 1979 Merseyside County Council saved it.

The 2,350-seat space was extended across Coal Street, the small side road that once separated it from the Legs of Man public house, and a new extension was added on the site of the former pub.

My first ever gig: The Jam at The Empire by Ian Prowse

It was a Wednesday night in Liverpool, November 1st, 1978 and I was 14 years old.

Paul Weller walked out onto the Liverpool Empire stage, pencil thin, sharp all-black suit, black shirt, bright green tie and Jam shoes. He plugged in his

bright red flashing Rickenbacker blade, slashed at it a few times and bellowed into the microphone: "Seen you before, I know your sort, you think the world awaits your every breath…"

And that was that. All was changed utterly in that instant. It's never been unchanged either – whatever alchemy took place within my teenage self at that very moment, it hit so hard, so deeply and with such force, that it's still the artistic fuel I'm running on 38 years later.

My first ever gig was The Jam and, just like your first match when you emerge from within the stands and see the green pitch for the first time, your first concert never leaves you – it's outside of all your previous experiences. The noise, the lights, the massive PA and the theatre of it all (punk poet Patrik Fitzgerald and cartoon act The Dickies were the supports).

It wasn't just The Jam's gigs that affected me so profoundly – I attended another five Jam concerts, including the infamous blood bath that was the first

48

Deeside Leisure Centre show – it was the songs and, in particular, Paul Weller's words. He was singing about me and my world: working class, council estate kid, parochial, resentful, in awe of the nearby big city… but, most of all, teenage. My overriding memory of the gigs was how teenage they were: I don't recall any old people (by old, I mean over 23). It really was all about the kids.

This Is The Modern World was my first album, the lyrics at the top of this piece were my road to Damascus moment and, listening to it on my terrible little cassette recorder, by the time he sings the expletives with such rage and venom, I was a goner.

If the Liverpool Empire gig had made me want to be in a band months earlier in 1978, the songs themselves were like missives from the one who understood us… our leader.

I was too young and uncool to realise that much of this era Jam had been appropriated from The Clash and that all became irrelevant two days after the Empire gig, when they released All Mod Cons, a masterpiece. The backwards guitar coda to In The Crowd can still reduce me to tears, Down In The Tube Station At Midnight is still the bench mark for all lyric writers and Mr. Clean still does punk anger better than punk did – and it's the best song ever written by anybody about the class war. They still copied The Clash, but this time brilliantly, on A Bomb In Wardour Street and Weller also did the unthinkable and put acoustic love songs on the record: English Rose and Fly… good God, he knew our working class angst was complicated by our feelings for girls, too!

He was 20… the bastard. Then they had a genuine hit single on the next album, Eton Rifles, and became massive. I kinda got off the bus at that point, as I couldn't stand all the nerds getting into my band. Privately, of course, I loved them as much as ever and bought every single thing they put out: Liza Radley, Funeral Pyre, Ghosts, Scrape Away. They were better than ever, I was just being a divvy.

I love that they will never get back together. I love that Weller split them up when he did: at the very height of their fame and power. I love the righteousness of it all, his clear reasoning, brimming still with conviction. So brave. They were our Beatles… thank God, then, they never became our Rolling Stones.

By October 1979, £330,000 had been spent on the backstage, in time for two Queen gigs in December that year. Journalist David Banks came from North Wales to see them play.

"I was a child living in North Wales so we only ever came to Liverpool for shopping trips or the annual visit to the panto," he says. "The Queen gig in November 1979 was my first experience of live music on this scale.

"Queen were at the Liverpool Empire on their Crazy Tour - they had been starting to do stadiums, but this was a tour of smaller venues.

"They played their greatest hits up to that point - Keep Yourself Alive, Now I'm Here, Brighton Rock - with Brian May's extended guitar solo, '39, Love of My Life, Killer Queen and, of course, Bohemian Rhapsody.

"It was denim as far as the eye could see. I went with three of my friends, all of us 14, dropped off outside the Empire by a parent. As soon as we got in the shouts went up of 'Wally' from the crowd. We were in the circle, with a great view. Queen had a new crane mounted lightshow which added to the spectacle. It was stupendously loud, an overwhelming spectacle for a 14-year-old's first-ever rock gig. My ears were ringing for days. Nothing I have seen since has ever matched that gig.

"Freddie was at the height of his powers, Queen were the world's greatest rock band - arguably - and he had the crowd in the palm of his hand. One minute belting out numbers like Tie Your Mother Down, the next gently dueting with the audience on Love of My Life.

"There was no-one like him then, and there's never been anyone to match him since. He was the original and the greatest, completely crazy, and we loved him."

The improvements at the theatre continued, with a further £350,000 investment in 1980. This included new lighting facilities, sound system and new dressing rooms.

The day I rode in a lift with Kate Bush, by Mark Thomas

One of the best things about being a news reporter is that you never quite know when you go to the office in the morning how your working day will turn out. You are frequently surprised, sometimes shocked, and just occasionally delighted by the events that unfold.

One of those days of delight began for me as a routine day shift on the Liverpool Echo - but would be etched into my memory forever as the day I met Kate Bush.

It was the morning of April 3, 1979, and Kate was in Liverpool preparing to make her stage debut, at the start of her first and, as it transpired only live tour to date. The Tour of Life was to take in 24 dates across Europe over the next six weeks, and featured music from her first two albums, The Kick Inside and Lionheart.

It being her first performance, her live career was to be launched with a press conference at Liverpool's Atlantic Tower Hotel. And I was asked by the newsdesk to pop along.

Still just 20 years old, Kate had stormed to the top of the charts with Wuthering Heights a year earlier, becoming, at 19, the first woman to have a number one UK hit with a self-penned song.

She had massive appeal among girls, who were fascinated by her ethereal beauty, unique sense of style and haunting songs, and among boys, for whom her lithe body, sensuous dance routines and startling eyes aroused passions of a quite different order.

I had just turned 23 myself, and was by no means immune to her attractions, having been as captivated as millions of others by her Top of the Pops appearances performing hits like Wow and The Man with the Child in His Eyes.

The Kate Bush I encountered at the press conference was, on the face of it, a very young 20-year-old, speaking in a high-pitched voice with a distinctive London accent, and clearly nervous at the prospect of facing a live audience for the first time.

Yet when she talked, it was with a maturity and depth that was at odds with her demeanour. A journalist asked her to explain the meaning of the lyrics of The Kick Inside, the song which gave her first album its name. She said she had written it as a teenager, and it told the story of a Victorian girl who has had an incestuous relationship with her brother, writing her suicide note to him after discovering that she has fallen pregnant and electing to take her own life to spare him from disgrace. You could have heard a pin drop in the room.

As we were leaving, one of Kate's entourage asked me if I was looking forward to the concert, and I replied that unfortunately I did not have a ticket. He reached into a pocket and handed me two free tickets for the show - gold dust basically, given that devoted fans had queued for hours to get tickets for the sell-out concert when they had gone on sale three months earlier. I travelled down in the lift with the press officer, another aide, and Kate herself. Occasionally I have been asked for a trivia fact about myself that would surprise people, and my regular response has been "I once travelled in a lift with Kate Bush".

The concert that night was an extraordinary occasion. Kate's renditions of her songs were carefully choreographed, dramatic performances, accompanied by dancers. Headset radio mics are commonplace today, but were unheard of in 1979. Kate pretty much pioneered them that night, wearing a headset fashioned from a wire coat hanger that allowed her to perform her energetic dance routines with both arms free as she sang into the attached radio microphone. Her physical fitness levels must have been extraordinary, given how powerfully she was able to sing as she danced, with no sign of breathlessness.

The concert was a fully-fledged piece of performance art, including magical illusions arranged and performed by magician Simon Drake, dramatic lighting, and myriad costume changes to fit the mood of her songs. The treatment brilliantly brought to life on stage evocative songs like Hammer Horror, Oh England My Lionheart, Coffee Homeground and Wow.

She did not speak to the audience during the per-

formance, which only served to add to the magical atmosphere it conjured. In terms of imaginative presentation and performance, this show was in a league of its own, a world away from the wild and dangerous performances of the rock bands of the era, every move and gesture planned with surgical precision to extract the maximum effect. It was intricate, meticulous even, but the result was in no sense mechanical, having a beauty and flow to it that was quite mesmerising to behold.

Her encore and final song, inevitably Wuthering Heights, had the auditorium in raptures.

The show ended to wild audience acclaim, and at last Kate broke the fourth wall to thank us, sobbing with emotion. "I will never forget tonight," she said. Neither, I suspect, will any of us lucky enough to have been there. None of us, of course, could have known then that after this tour she would not perform live on stage again for another 35 years. Liverpool hosted many extraordinary gigs in the 1970s and '80s, but this night was to prove to be a collector's item indeed.

Cutting a dash in seventies Britain

Chapter 7

Victoria Street, Dale Street and down by the waterfront

The Royal Tiger Club

Many of the clubs that we talk about in Dirty Stop Outs have long since gone. Some of the buildings remain, in other uses, but many have been demolished. But it's unusual to find a whole street that's vanished too, as is the case for Manchester Street.

This little side street, which ran by the entrance to the Birkenhead tunnel, was home to an infamous members only adult cinema back in the '70s, known as the Gilmore Adult Cinema Club, which burnt down in 1985.

It was also home to the first News From Nowhere shop and a Yates' Wine Lodge, frequented by the cool Eric's crowd - Ian McCulloch, Julian Cope and friends. Channel 4's The Tube filmed them here in the early '80s.

But its most popular resident in the '70s was the Royal Tiger, frequented by journalists from the nearby ECHO and Daily Post offices in their old offices on Victoria Street and, professional footballers, their wives and managers. It was also reported to have attracted musicians including Kenny Ball and Acker Bilk.

Joan Kelly remembers it well. "It was on the corner of Victoria Street, at the turn for Manchester Street. It was very popular in my day. We used to go to Tracy's in Stanley Street then onto Tiger. It had a downstairs as well.

"When it was first open the footballers went, then just the townies."

Bernie Monaghan also remembers the football crowd. He adds: "The Tiger used to open in the afternoons when the pubs shut at 3pm. The footballers would go in after training."

Dunk Davis was one of the DJs at the Royal Tiger.

"Liverpool was a fantastic place to have a night out in those days," he says. "I started at The Royal Tiger Club in Manchester Street in 1973. I worked with some of the best entertainers in the world. The music I played was Motown and soul and USA funk bands - I was on all the mailing lists so got them before anyone else. I was very well known on Merseyside and building my name as a DJ in all the night clubs over the year through the '70s.

51

"After we finished work at the Royal Tiger we all went to the Pier Head until about 3am, and to the Hole in the Wall where we got red hot soup and a butty because it was open all night.

"I never went out much - I was always working - but did go to the She club and the Wooky Holllow if I had a night off. They were fab clubs with great DJs.

"I was also guest compere at the Wispa club in Liverpool and worked on the very first Beatles convention with Billy Butler at Mr Pickwick's Club."

The She Club

Long before The Living Room, and now the Sugar Hut, Victoria Street's hottest place to be was The She Club.

With several floors of music, and a strict door policy, it was the place to be.

John Lawson remembers it with fondness. "It was like a local: everyone from the owner down to the cloakroom lady were friendly, there was never any trouble.

"The disco in the basement played great music, thanks to Tom Day the DJ, there was a restaurant on the top floor, and on the ground floor there were live acts on six days a week - acts like the Foundations, Johnny Nash, and the Platters all appeared on there, and as for the women ... well I'll keep that to myself!"

Phil Hough had an unusual method of getting round the She door policy of a tie for all gentlemen. "I remember going to the She club in Dale Street and we would have a few across the road in the wine lodge," he recalls. "Someone said 'You won't get in without a tie on'. At 9pm on a Saturday night where do you buy a tie?

"Well for a small tip the barman used to cut the shape of a tie out of the pink football ECHO and pin it to your shirt, so it looked to the bouncers that you had one on.

"I tried it, the bouncer laughed and said 'Oy! What's that? Ah get in lad, nice one'. I then found out you could remove your tie as soon as you were in."

The club was also popular with staff from other venues around town, who were invited for an unofficial late-night drink after hours.

Phil laughs: "It was a meeting place for many of the other clubs owners and bouncers and so it had stay behinds. After the 2am kick out other people would start walking in and a special room would open up with a bar area. Invited people would go in.

"I got in only once. And just my luck, a police raid happened. They took my beer off me and labelled it up and took my name. I never heard anything, but it closed down eventually."

Probe Records

Founded in 1971 by Geoff Davies, the shop was originally located on Clarence Street, off Brownlow Hill

The Other Place on Stanley Street.
Photo: John Harrison

with a second location soon opened in the basement of Silly Billies clothes shop.

But its most famous incarnation was after its 1976 relocation to Button Street, just around the corner from Eric's Club on Mathew Street.

Thanks to a staff which, at various times, included Julian Cope, Pete Burns (with his wife Lynn), and Paul Rutherford, it found itself at the centre of the city's emerging punk and new wave music scene.

Gary Shelley was a regular at Probe. He says: "Pete Burns - as is well documented - worked at Probe and would sit on the floor with black contact lenses. Very scary, a great way of ignoring you which he often did, even if you wanted to buy something. Officially the worst salesman ever.

"The biggest worry we had was not damaging your latest purchase from Probe while jumping up and down like a loon in Eric's."

In order to supplement the takings in the shop itself, Geoff also set up an independent wholesale arm of the business, through which he would promote up and coming talent. Many larger record retailers throughout the north-west of England such as HMV, Virgin Records and Our Price bought most of their independent label stock from Probe.

The business became successful enough to eventually set up its own record label. Initially called simply Probe Records, it was re-branded Probe Plus in order to avoid confusion between the retail shop and the record label. The decision of which bands and musicians to sign up to the label was a collaboration between Geoff Davies and two friends, writer Andrew Kenyon-Smith and DJ John Peel.

By the '90s, the shop had again relocated, this time to Slater Street off Bold Street around the corner from The Zanzibar on Seel Street, where it stayed until 2010 before moving to Bluecoat Chambers on School Lane in the centre of the city.

Tiffany's

Julie Fadden says: "Tiffany's was on the corner of Fenwick Street, you went downstairs and there was a fence around it at ground level.

"It was fab. All the Childwall College discos were there - always a great night, fab music, many happy memories waiting to dance with your chosen one."

Mitch Poole agrees: "Tiffany's was under India Buildings and always used for Childwall College's parties. Was anyone actually allowed in if you were over 16?"

George Jones adds: "Tiffany's had strippers on at lunch time for the office workers around there - or so I believe!"

The Other Place

Philip Campbell remembers a late night – and early morning – in this Stanley Street club . **"I went the Other Place, fell asleep in the toilets, woke up and the club was empty," he says. "Fell asleep on one of the long seats, and a cleaner woke me up. I rose like Dracula coming out of his coffin - never heard a scream so loud! Poor woman nearly fainted on the spot."**

The Victoriana

Julie Ray (nee Stephens) remembers great nights at The Victoriana on Victoria Street. "It was the best club around for music - in that they cared about it. When I used to go it specialised in Tamla Motown and soul, bands like Temptations. Great dancing there. It was a bit of a forerunner of the Northern Soul scene which was to spring up a few years later in Wigan."

It was one of the many clubs which changed its name during the decade. Joan Kelly recalls: "The Victoriana in Victoria Street was previously called The Downbeat, Hotsy Totsy was also previously called the Latin Quarter."

Ma Boyle's Oyster Bar

This business district favourite moved from one historic home in 1974, and found itself another. Ma Boyle's Oyster Bar was established in 1870 at 2 Old Hall Street, but it had to move when Moorfields station opened, and found a new home in the Tower Building.

It was a much-loved bar, with an annual Beaujolais run and its famous fresh oysters.

Its customers followed it, and after a brief closure a couple of years ago, it's now back open (minus the Oyster Bar tag) and business is booming.

ONLY A FEW TICKETS LEFT FOR
BLACK OAK'S 3RD U.K. TOUR

AT BLACK OAK ARKANSAS' SPECIAL REQUEST, TICKETS FOR THEIR CONCERT ARE KEPT TO THE MINIMAL PRICE OF £1

BLACK OAK ARKANSAS: They're hot, they're nasty, and they're gonna make you scream for more.
Black Oak Arkansas on tour
with ... guests **SASSAFRAS**.

... Centre   22 February   Southend, Kursaal Ballroom
... versity   23 Feb...

BANDOLIER
BUDGIE

A DEVASTATING NEW ALBUM

BUDGIE ON TOUR

10 SEPT/MANCHESTER—FREE TRADE HALL   22 SEPT/BARNSTABLE—QUEENS HALL
11 SEPT/PRESTON—GUILDHALL   24 SEPT/YEOVIL—JOHNSON HALL
12 SEPT/HANLEY (STOKE)—VICTORIA HALLS   25 SEPT/PENZANCE—THE GARDENS
...AMPTON—COUNTY GROUND   27 SEPT/CROMER—LINKS PAVILION
                                        31 SEPT/LONDON—ROUNDHOUSE

CAPTAIN
TRIAD Presents
BEEF HEART
Tickets 75p from Cosmopolitan One-Stop

Liverpool Stadium
Mon. April 3rd
7:30pm

Tickets on sale at door

degro posters

54

Asgard Enterprises Ltd. present

HAWKWIND

Saturday
14th July 1973
7-30 p.m.

Tickets 99p
(inc. VAT)

No: 2375

Chapter 8
Liverpool Stadium

Long before Liverpool had an arena, it played host to a stadium, where boxing and wrestling nights mixed with an impressive list of gigs.

Built in the early 1930s at a cost of £30,000 - and only demolished in the late 1980s - it was tucked away on Bixteth Street, in the area that backs onto Old Hall Street and Tithebarn Street.

First and foremost a boxing venue, it served a number of functions over its 50-odd years. Winston Churchill chose the stadium to launch the Conservatives' election campaign in 1951 and trade unions regularly used it to meet with their members.

But it was for gigs that it attracted most of its big names. Louis Armstrong was its first music star in 1956, and four years later, it was the birthplace of Merseybeat - with The Beatles sitting in the audience.

In 1960 Eddie Cochran and Gene Vincent had been due to appear at the stadium as part of a package tour that had created a sensation amongst UK rock 'n' roll fans.

Before the Liverpool gig, tragedy had struck. Cochran had been killed in a car accident, and Vincent injured. The gig still went ahead, despite his injuries, and he was supported by up and coming Liverpool bands Gerry and the Pacemakers, alongside Bob Evans and the Five Shillings.

It was supposedly after this that Lennon asked Alan Williams to start getting The Beatles proper gigs, meaning in venues like Liverpool Stadium.

Another early Beatles connection came in the form of the venue's owner, Best Enterprises, run by British Army former middleweight boxing champion Johnny Best Senior, grandfather of one Pete Best, the original Beatles drummer.

For the rest of the '60s it was mostly used for boxing, apart from The Kaleidoscope Festival in December 1968, headlined by Pink Floyd, with support from The Move and local act The Klubs.

By the time the '70s dawned, another key player on the city's music scene had taken an interest in Liverpool Stadium.

In 1970 Roger Eagle, who was later to play a huge part in Liverpool's punk and post-punk scene, started to book bands for the stadium. His ear for music and eye for a good deal meant that they were soon getting some of the best up and coming bands on the circuit.

Having worked as a DJ at the Twisted Wheel in Manchester, he had good contacts, and a new ethos.

As he said to the Liverpool Echo in 1970: "My own personal profit is about 5% of the takings. The groups get 70% as opposed to the 50 or 60% most promoters offer. We don't believe in pushing people around so we don't have a DJ on telling them what to do.

"If they want they can dance in the aisles and move out of their seats. That's why we don't have reserved seats, so people feel they can move if they want."

Eagle worked under the name Triad Productions, and set about bringing some of the best acts to the venue.

This began in September 1970 when he put on stellar line up of Free, Mott The Hoople, Bronco and Trees.

The following year Free returned, alongside Hawkwind, Yes, Led Zeppelin, The Who, The Faces, Mott the Hoople and T. Rex.

Phil Hough talks Led Zeppelin, Liverpool Stadium and a chance meeting with The Who

"I went to see Led Zeppelin twice in Liverpool in 1971. First gig was on May 10 at the Students Union De Montfort Hall, Mount Pleasant, and the second at Liverpool Stadium on November 29. I was 18.

"I took my girlfriend (now my wife) to see both shows, and the De Montfort Hall show was all standing and we were all in one massive mosh pit. It was fantastic.

"The stadium was not a great gig venue, they had great bands on there but it was a dump, it was not stewarded good either and nobody cared what you did so it was great to jump around and dance. Funny enough I took my best mate Willy to this gig as well. He had only heard about them from me, and I will never forget his face when Robert Plant hit the high notes of the opening Immigrant Song. He was gob smacked and legged it straight to the front in mad reverie.

"They did have some tech issues that night, sound quality problems. I remember the arrogance of Plant and Page telling us it was a dump and they would give this place a miss in future, quite the opposite to the lovely John Paul Jones, who was the perfect gentleman. I remember Jimmy Page playing the guitar with a cello bow. It was a fantastic night.

"I was an apprentice at Carlett Park College at the time, and Monday, May 14, 1971, we got the word that The Who had turned up in Liverpool and asked if they could play the students' union that night. No prior advertising and no tickets, just turn up and pay on the door. So we left college immediately and when we arrived there was a queue about a mile out of the union entrance with a piece of A4 paper on the front door saying, 'The Who Tonight 8pm'. It was a sunny day and I remember a white Rolls Royce slowly driving past. The tinted window came down and a smiling Roger Daltry gave us a wave as we were sitting on the pavement. They played the whole of their latest album that night, the marvellous Who's Next. Unbelievable."

Dave Roberts from Wallasey remembers it well: "I started by going to concerts there around 1971. I think Led Zeppelin was the first gig I ever went to there.

"The atmosphere there was amazing, people used to arrive there in the early afternoon and sit around outside. The venue attracted mainly a hippy audience and they dressed accordingly in T-shirts and loons."

Dave became such a fan of the bands he saw that he started working at the stadium.

"I used to go around the back of the venue and used to ask the band's crews if they needed any help in getting their gear in," he explains.

"This led to me being asked to work there.

"One of my favourite gigs has to be Hawkwind when they recorded their Space Ritual album. Other stand out gigs would be Can, Amon Duul II, Faust, Tangerine Dream, Led Zeppelin, Arthur Brown's Kingdom Come, Gong, Rory Gallagher and Thin Lizzy.

"Roger Eagle was an amazing guy to work for. I had several jobs there. I used to help build the stage over the wrestling ring.

"If it was a big gig we would go there Friday night after the wrestling and work through the night building the stage.

"I would also have a stall for Roger selling his bootleg LPs and other bits and pieces, and then lock up at night after the gigs.

"I was working there one night and Roger asked me to come down to his new club which was called Revolution then. He asked me to do front of house security for The Runaways. "That was an amazing gig."

The following year, 1972, saw another gig from Free, as well as shows from Jethro Tull, Hawkwind (twice), Mott the Hoople (twice), Lindisfarne, Camel, two dates from David Bowie, Roxy Music, Mountain, The Kinks and Wishbone Ash.

As part of Mott the Hoople's Rock 'n' Roll Circus tour that year - when admission was 70p - music hall comedian Max Wall did the band's warm-up slot.

The stadium differed from other venues in Liverpool at the time as gig goers would hang around outside the building for hours prior to the doors opening. As there were no age restrictions, under-age drinkers who were unable to get served in one of various pubs

nearby - of which only The Cross Keys, a favourite haunt of journalists from the Liverpool Echo and Daily Post, remains - used to get their drinks from the off-license on St. Paul's Square and sit outside all afternoon, as long as the weather permitted.

The underground music scene in the city was especially strong at the time with Probe Records selling many of the alternative music papers.

Captain Beefheart first appeared at The Stadium in April 1972 - a performance that coincided with an exhibition of his art at Bluecoat Chambers.

Be Bop Deluxe and the Doctors of Madness, as remembered by David King

The Liverpool Stadium was a strange kind of venue for rock bands. Not quite as prestigious as its neighbour, the Liverpool Empire, it catered mainly for up and coming bands who hadn't yet made the big time.

The bands played on top of the boxing ring with the PA and Lighting systems set either side of the ring. The sound was terrible and the venue had high ceilings so you had lots of natural echo. But the entrance fee was always cheap and the pub across the road served alcohol to underage gig-goers like me.

I went to see Be Bop Deluxe and the Doctors of Madness at Liverpool Stadium on February 8 ,1976. I'd previously seen them performing their new single Ships in the Night on the TV show Supersonic which aired around 5pm just as I was getting in from school. They were not the typical long-haired rock band that were around at the time instead sporting short haircuts and playing a mixture of funky rock and pop.

In the '70s support bands got a raw deal from Liverpool audiences. They were fair game to be booed or bottled off and tonight's victims, The Doctors of Madness, were no exceptions. The Doctors came onto a mysterious intro with a Vincent Price type narration claiming the Doctors put sharks into swimming pools and practiced brain surgery. They were a pre-punk outfit comprising four members. The blue-haired singer played guitar and antagonised the audience at every opportunity.

They had the usual bass and drums plus an eerie violinist who gave them a Velvet Underground type of sound, and I loved them.

They were well ahead of the game and in 1976 gave a taste of what punk would bring in 1977 with the explosion of the Sex Pistols.

Thankfully the main act seemed to get a better reception.

Be Bop Deluxe came on stage with a much better sound mix and elaborate lighting and stage equipment in the form of a perplex tube that lifted up in the air to present the band.

Bill Nelson was a great performer and a magnificent guitarist. They had a funky black bass player and a virtuoso keyboard player. The Stadium was only three quarters full that night as both bands were still up and coming.

It's down in history as a legendary gig and after that tour the two bands never performed together again going their separate ways and reaching nominal success. But it's a gig everybody now wishes they had attende

In 1973 the Stadium had yet more Led Zeppelin, Focus, Deep Purple, Nazareth, Curved Air, and return shows from Wishbone Ash and Mott the Hoople.

In 1974, notable shows included Golden Earring, Bad Company, Nazareth, Barclay James Harvest, Thin Lizzy and Curved Air, with yet more Hawkwind in 1975, alongside Dr. Feelgood.

"The Dr. Feelgood gig was electrifying," recalls Dave Roberts.

"Everyone went wild as it was the first time they played there. The first six rows of seats were completely destroyed. It was a completely different crowd for that gig."

Dave worked at the stadium from 1973 to 1976.

"From 1973 to 1975 I was at art college studying graphic design so didn't go out much during the week," he says. "I lived in Wallasey so spent a lot of time there. I got involved in working at the Watchfield

festival in 1975 and the Seasalter Festival in 1976 building the stages and working as stage crew.

"By that time the venue was running down as they were planning to demolish the Stadium.

"I never really worked at Eric's, but would go there on a regular basis. One of the stand out gigs for me was Iggy Pop in 1979. I also enjoyed Stiff Little Fingers and Generation X."

Roger's future Eric's collaborator Ken Testi remembers when the gigs came to a close at The Stadium.

"Roger Eagle made a modest living managing shows for national promoters at Liverpool Stadium," says Ken. "He would sometimes promote his own shows at clubs around the city.

"We had met previously, but I began working with him when he asked Deaf School to perform at Le Metro.

"We did a number of shows together and got on pretty well. At the beginning of 1976 it became clear that the Stadium would soon close, I was aware that my tenure as Deaf School tour manager would soon end.

"Roger and I would soon both be out of work. His experience was at a limited number of venues with many bands and my experience was with a limited number of bands at many venues, there was a dovetailing of sorts."

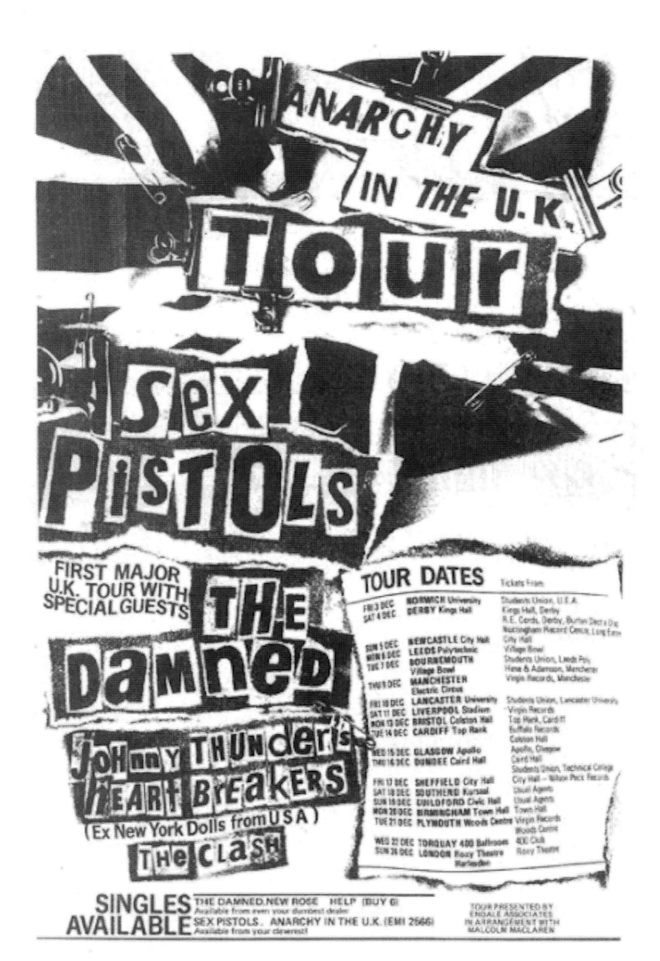

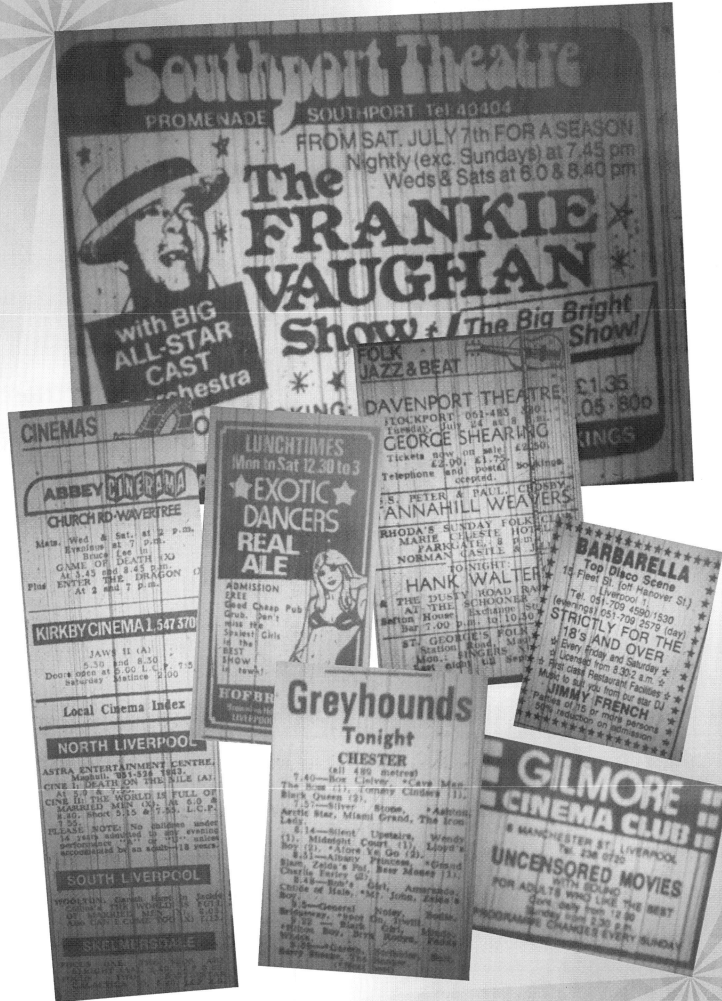

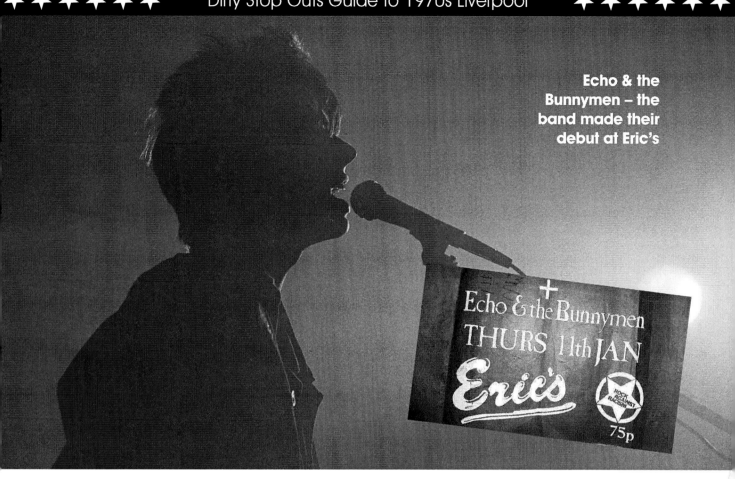

Echo & the Bunnymen – the band made their debut at Eric's

Chapter 9

Eric's

Roy Adams had opened the New Cavern in the old fruit exchange on the opposite side of Mathew Street from the original club. But it was far from the success of its namesake.

As Ken Testi remembers: "Roy re-configured the premises into two clubs. Gatsby's had its entrance on Victoria Street and was at street level. The basement opened onto Mathew Street and was called the Revolution.

"Neither was doing well when Roger (Eagle) and I started looking for club premises.

"We reached an agreement with Roy to do shows on Friday nights in the street level Gatsby's. A month later he persuaded us to move downstairs."

The basement was to become another of the most iconic clubs in music history - Eric's. Like The Cavern, it was to see the birth of a musical scene which would see Liverpool leading the way culturally again. And, like The Cavern in its day, it would see musicians as often in the crowds as on the stage.

On 1 October, 1976, Eric's opened its doors. On the bill that night were The Stranglers. Entrance was 60p, and in the audience were Ian McCulloch and Pete Wylie.

The club became a home for the weird and wonderful, with all genres welcome - from jazz, to reggae and folk to performance art and poetry, and especially punk.

The name, apparently, was chosen as a contrast to the glitzier clubs with their girls' names - places like Tiffany's and Samantha's.

DJ and promoter Marc Jones is the curator of Eric's to EVOL, a unique project looking at Liverpool's social history through its music and clubs.

"I think the point of Eric's in terms of social history is that it came out of nowhere, a year zero moment," he explains.

"Punk rock was born out of frustration, a hopelessness and anger directed at Britain and its failure to build on the promise of the '60s.

"Years of economic decline, high unemployment and weak governments made Britain a bleak place to live in the late '70s. So in real terms it wasn't surprising that punk rock happened... it was a big bang moment. Or a little bang moment!

"A whole set of individuals and misfits bored of pompous stadium rockers like Emerson Lake and

Eric's Doreen Allen

Palmer, Yes and even Rod Stewart, sort of sneaked and somehow found their way to clubs like Eric's all around the country, where this new music and movement was taking place.

"When you look at Liverpool now, you have no idea how grim it was in Liverpool right into the 1980s. There were many 'no go' areas in the city.

"Eric's happened at exactly the right time and exactly the right place."

Eric's was created with an open door policy on the acts that played, encouraging new bands to form and perform their first gigs.

Under the watchful eyes of Roger Eagle, Ken Testi and Pete Fulwell many bands played their first gigs, and got a taste of what it was like to perform live.

They also started a record company under the Eric's banner, and produced the Last Trumpet fanzine, and industry bible More or Less.

Ken remembers: "My favourite gigs would include the Runaways, which generated the biggest queue that Mathew Street has ever seen and brought us to the attention of national booking agents, making all that followed possible.

"I would also include Stanley Clarke for whom we had Mathew Street closed to accommodate both of Richard Branson's Manor mobile studios to record a live album."

Eric's played host to gigs from almost any genre - the policy was that if bands were good, they'd get on, no matter what their style. But it's the punk gigs it's possibly best-known for today.

Marc Jones adds: "Punk was so small and you have to remember 1976 was really only London and the odd gigs across the country.

"Eric's opened in late 1976 and even though the Sex Pistols played there it was to about 40 people and

half of them were Liverpool University students. In 1977 punk exploded as a movement, especially when the likes of the Clash, Ramones, Damned, Siouxsie and the Banshees and the Slits started gigging regularly and when they played Liverpool for the first time it was at Eric's.

"The thing I love about the early punk years was the whole DIY ethos, the bin bag and safety pin approach to design and fashion and indeed music... everybody was an individual, a rejection and a two fingered 'up yours' of traditional values and dressing smart to go out. And while most people could never afford a Vivienne Westwood punk cheese cloth bondage shirt or mohair... they could go to extraordinary lengths to shock and thrill in equal measures and people looked amazing in homemade dresses, second hand store clothes, army surplus, ripped up stuff, mums' and dads' stuff and a ton of imagination."

The glamorous gatekeeper - Doreen Allen

She was the face of Eric's, with her striking blonde hair and keen eye for new talent. Doreen Allen had been running things behind the scenes at Merseyside's clubs and gig venues for years, but it was Eric's that really made her name - written on so many of the club's iconic membership cards.

"I used to do the door most nights," she explains. "I worked for Roger at The Stadium until he went on to open Eric's in 1976.

"At first the Eric's office was in Probe and I helped out in there and did various jobs in Eric's - cloakroom, kitchen and the door.

"Then in 1977 the office was moved to the club and

I then worked full time in the office dealing with the memberships and the day to day running of the club."

On the door she was the gatekeeper of the night, the door diva who knew everyone on the scene.

"My first promotion was in the '60s when me and two friends put on three of Birkenhead's top bands at Westbourne Road, West Kirby Church Hall. A couple of years later in 1969 I started promoting bands like U.F.O and Judas Priest at O'Connors Tavern in Hardman Street, Liverpool. It was there that I met Roger Eagle who came along with a band called Greasy Bear - members of which later joined Sad Cafe and Duritti Column. Roger asked me to work for him when he started promoting at The Liverpool Stadium, which I did when I stopped putting the bands on at O'Connors."

Doreen's spot in the office was a regular haunt for bands, who'd pop in to see how tickets were going and to have a chat.

63

Striking fashions on show at Eric's

"I became friendly with Pete Wylie and Mac (Echo and the Bunnymen's Ian McCulloch) who hung around the club at lunchtimes, as it was open between 12pm and 2pm for people to buy tickets and membership cards - of which I signed a fair few," she laughs.

When she had a minute, Doreen would make time to see the bands who played Eric's, watching some of the biggest acts of the '70s.

She says: "My favourite gigs at Eric's were The Cramps and B-52s. Ian Drury was one of the nicest people to play Eric's but I do remember Elvis Costello being rather snotty!"

It was a scene with its own distinctive style, personified by Pete Burns and his wife Lynne, who ran a clothes shop out of Probe Records and gave the best haircuts in the city.

Doreen remembers fondly: "In those days none of us had much money to spend on clothes and I remember Paul Rutherford used to make some of mine. Later on I did used to go to London shopping with Pete Burns at Kensington Market and World's End.

"After Eric's closed in 1980 I went on to become labels manageress of Eric's/Inevitable Records and my office was above Cafe Tabac, Bold Street.

"I also managed Dead or Alive and Ponderosa Glee Boys for a time. I was also working on the door at The Warehouse and Club Zoo.

"Then in 1983 I started Planet X and also ran The Frankie Goes to Hollywood fan club.

"My memory of the closure of Eric's was being handed a Customs and Excise Notice in the daytime then the police raid at night."

The roster of national groups who played Eric's reads like a who's who of brilliant '70s music, from The Jam to The Stranglers and Blondie to The Clash. Many bands, such as The Police and The Sex Pistols, played right at the start of their careers.

But it was arguably the local acts which were most influenced by Eric's and its ethos. Bands such as OMD, Echo and the Bunnymen, The Teardrop Explodes and Wah! Heat all played their first gigs there. Big In Japan were another Eric's success story, before its members went on to influence popular music - and culture more widely - to this day as The Lightning Seeds, Frankie Goes to Hollywood, Siouxsie and the Banshees, the KLF, and the founder of the Cream nightclub.

Andy McCluskey and Paul Humphreys formed OMD for a one-off show at Eric's, but thanks to Pete Fulwell's introduction to Factory Records they went on to huge success. Andy later went on to run Motor Museum Studios, inspiring a whole generation of young musicians himself.

As well as musicians, Eric's was home to a creative scene of artists, photographers, designers and writers.

"There has always been a need for social misfits, musicians, artists, writers, designers and just weirdos to gather like moths around the darkened lights and dark places in subterranean night clubs and old back street warehouses," says Marc. "What made Eric's so remarkable was that such a set of individuals and scenesters... like a punk Orpheus and his girlfriend Eurydice, they descended into that underworld and later emerged out of it in a set of bands that had such an impact on modern music across the world espe-

cially in the early to mid '80s.

"Eric's, Bradys, Plato's Ballroom, System, Warehouse, Planet X, Lomax, Le Bateau, Evol, Korova and Kazimier - the underground is always there. It just changes with style, music, fashion but I always think it will attract the same types of people.

"Eric's crowd changed fairly rapidly. The real early adopters and scene heads were true punks, no uniforms, no stereotyping, be whatever you want to be but have fun doing it.

"Punk became a uniform later on but as somebody pointed out to me, in the beginning Eric's was a new music club, it was not a punk club.

"Roger Eagle loved blues, jazz, reggae and rock, it was just so many of these punk and new wave bands from the US and UK caught the zeitgeist perfectly. Timing was everything.

"But like in every great club, there is a clique, a hierarchy, a king, a queen... a whole court of different people who are possessive and bitchy and very protective of their club. Around them will be their friends, and the circle grows wider and wider and even in the underground there's small competing groups of musicians, trend setters and hangers on.

"There is almost a disdain for the general punter, especially if they turned up in flares and still had a sideburns and bum fluff. It is the dynamic of every club."

Marc has done extensive research on Liverpool's tribes of the time. "I have always loved tribes and I think it's one of the things I miss on the streets of Britain now because they were fantastic.

"I always think - even more so than that early punk

thing - growing up as a teenager in Liverpool in the early to mid '80s was perhaps the most exciting time because of the tribes, their rituals, their fashion and of course their music.

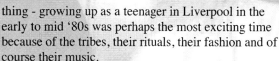

"I came to it in '82 or '83 but obviously grew up in the '70s. I would have loved to have seen the Clash, but I was queuing up to see Star Wars!"

Eric's rise was rapid. By the time it had been open for less than a year it was attracting the hottest new bands.

"By 1977 shows by the likes of the Clash and the Ramones were packed events and new people were attracted to the whole punk and new wave scene," says Marc.

"Roger Eagle had brilliant ears and booked so many brilliant bands but never had any money!

"As Doreen Allen, the club secretary and door girl, recalls that on a wet Tuesday in November, there could be one man and no dog watching Gang of Four or the Cure. She always said Roger was far happier when he was losing money but a great band had played.

"The matinees were a god send, where Roger could persuade the bands to play another show in the afternoon for a reduced fee to a room full of spotty teenagers."

Gary Shelley was a regular at Eric's, despite still being at school.

"Matinees were perfect. I was only about 15 and had a curfew. Saturday, spend a day around Probe Records then, at 5pm, gigs at Eric's.

"Generation X were fantastic live. Remember this one really well. Attended the matinee (not old enough to see the late show). Loved the sound they had, and Billy Idol was the star he was destined to be. What a cool, lovely guy he was.

"We spent a lot of time after the show chatting with them. They were brilliant. Like many of the bands then, very accessible in Eric's, usually mingling with the crowd.

"Killing Joke was another great gig. Love them. Power, passion, awesome. Original line up including Pig Youth. The intensity of Jaz Coleman was frightening at the time as a kid. Still one of my favourite bands. Often we didn't know what to expect when we turned up, there was just a name on the flyer, you hadn't heard of the band. This was Eric's for me, like a musical lucky bag! Anticipation, excitement, never knowing at times what you where going to get.

"We spent a good hour after the matinee in the tiny dressing room chatting with the band. Pig Youth possibly the smelliest person I've ever met. Great memories.

"The Modettes/Passions gig I remember as all a bit bleak, but I really liked The Passions. I'm In Love With The German Film Star was a semi-hit at one point. Modettes were slightly livelier and having a Lambretta at the time, I had to check them out.

"Then there was Spizz Energi - energi being the word. Lunatics would be a better word. Where's Captain Kirk? A classic that became one of my brother's favourites.

"Looking back there are so many bands I didn't get chance to see. This was due to a mixture of being told not to be home after 10pm by mum and dad, and my £7 a week not stretching that far. At this time we had so many opportunities to see bands that unless you had a decent paying job, you had to choose.

"The Mathew Street area is obviously now unrecognisable compared to what it was. It was just a moment in time. You were young, had no real worries (except standard teenage ones). It was a time which just happened to coincide with a great place, great bands … it really was the perfect cocktail.

"I was devastated when Eric's was forced to close.

"Yes I went on the march around the city centre to the chant of 'What do we want? We want Eric's!'.

"Brady's didn't last and nothing came close after that. The music scene changed and we spent the next few years trying to find somewhere even slightly as good as Eric's. Planet X, the Warehouse … good times, but nothing captured that time again."

Like all great things, Eric's days were sadly numbered.

In March 1980 it was raided by police. The final

acts that night was The Psychedelic Furs, supported by Wah! Heat, whose performance was recorded for a John Peel session.

After some minor drug offence arrests the club was closed for the rest of the evening. Customers protested, and even organised a march, but it didn't re-open as Eric's. A spell as Brady's lasted 12 months.

"All clubs have a golden few years and never last more than three or four years," says Marc.

"Most promoters live week by week, feast or famine, and once the bands have moved onto university tours, theatres and big shows …

"Scenes and bands constantly evolve and move around cities. Eric's had terrible problems with the VAT, with serious men calling at the door.

"Bands don't really make money on that scale, most break even or lose a bit of money. You'll get the occasional one that flies but two weeks later you'll have an absolute disaster. I have put on Oasis, Radiohead, Verve in the past and paid them between £50 and £300 quid, but the only one I made huge money on was Suede when they broke big. It's swings and roundabouts.

"Yes, it had hassle off the police and club was raided for drugs but this wasn't the dance and acid house years. What were they ever going to find?

"Who know who Eric's upset along the way? But better a punk club goes out with a bang rather than fizzling out with a whimper! It makes Eric's even more legendary and adds to the myth."

The Damned at Eric's, as remembered by Dave King

"Queuing up outside Eric's Club Matthew Street on a cold January Saturday night in 1979 was not for the faint-hearted! There was a cold wind blowing in from the Mersey, and an even colder reception came from the passing gangs of scallies heading across the car park to the Harrington Bar.

"Getting past the bouncers was the first test, as I was still only 17. But once you got past that hurdle you were nearly home and dry (or warm, in my case).

"Greeting you at the small ticket reception was either Doreen Allen or sometimes up-and-coming singer Jane Casey, who one time took my ticket money looking a frightful shade of yellow, as she was suffering from a recent bout of jaundice.

"You went down the steep stairs into the dark, damp basement that called itself Eric's. Straight to the bar to by two pints of watery bitter and then over to the jukebox. A quick look around to see who was in and we spotted Pete Burns sitting in the corner with his wife and entourage, which included soon-to-be Frankie Goes to Hollywood singer Holly Johnson.

"But the Damned were in town, and although they were not the most popular of the punk bands, they

Ian Broudie

were guaranteed to give you a laugh at least.

"The jukebox was spinning a heavy reggae track. Standing there looking very fearsome was the club owner Roger Eagle.

"We made our escape from Roger, straight to the front of the stage. Big mistake, as when the Damned came onstage and Rat Scabies hit his snare drum, there was a huge crowd push forward and I thought my ribs were going to burst out of my leather bike jacket. They played all their old songs and some of their new album Machine Gun Etiquette.

"Captain Sensible spent half the evening gobbing at the audience. Rat was a powerhouse on the drums. Dave Vanian was slowly turning gothic and the bass duties were performed by Algy Ward from the Australian punk band the Saints.

"As soon as the band finished their encore we made straight to the band dressing rooms, which were just right of the stage. I tried this after every gig but most band managers chased you out, but not tonight, as the Damned were in party mode and traded cans of beer with us for any jokes we could remember. At one point we were left alone with Rat Scabies, who produced a cheap looking yellow guitar and started strumming. My best friend Martin was saving up for a guitar and asked Rat if he wanted to sell it. Rat said it was his for a tenner, and Martin couldn't believe his luck.

"Give us a minute," said Rat. "I just want to go back onstage and mime to Public Image and then you can have it".

"Rat climbed onstage, which attracted the crowd back, and after shouts of "smash it!" Rat proudly gave the crowd what they wanted, and broke the yellow guitar in two against the Eric's backdrop.

"Rat came back into the dressing room and said to my friend, "The price has gone down. I'll take a fiver".

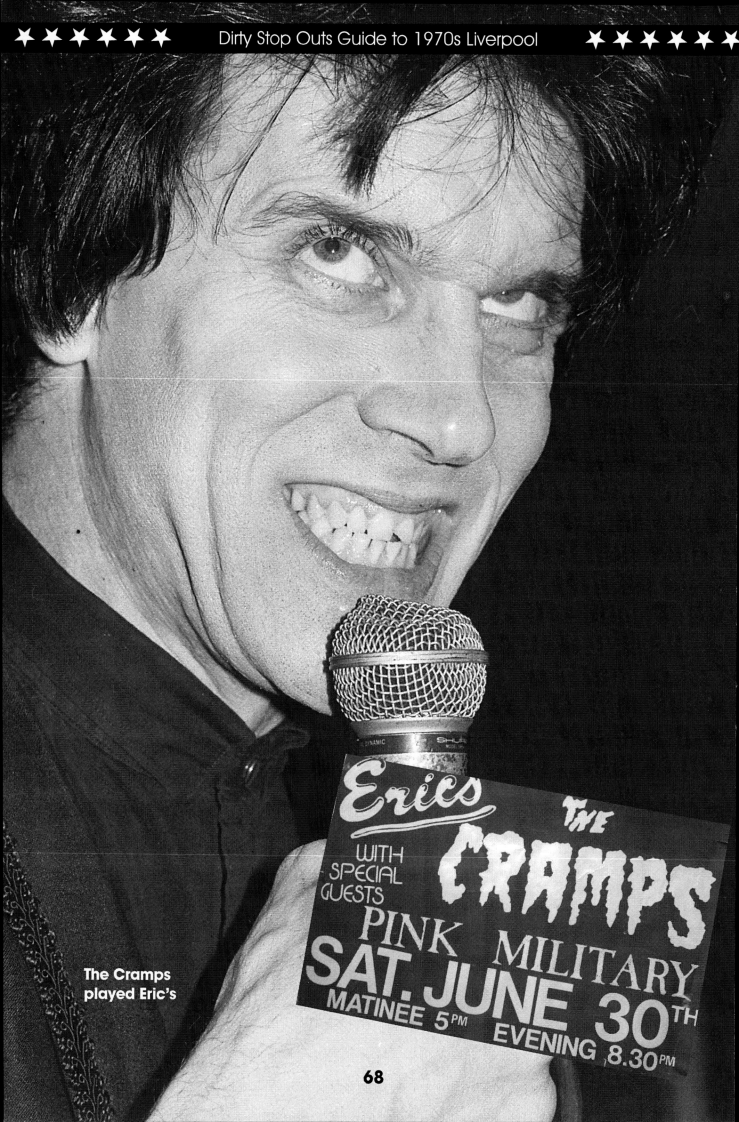

**The Cramps
played Eric's**

Erics THE CRAMPS
WITH SPECIAL GUESTS
PINK MILITARY
SAT. JUNE 30TH
MATINEE 5PM
EVENING 8.30PM

Thanks to Colin Evans
for this picture of his
night out at Wispa

Chapter 10
North of the city

Allinson's/Wispa

Cabaret was big in the '70s, and few places did it better than Allinson's Theatre Club on Church Road in Litherland.

The site previously had been the Regal Cinema and a bowling alley, but opened as Allinson's in July 1966, when club owner John Allinson bought it. It was initially a members-only club, although up to two guests could be signed in. Gentlemen had to wear collars, ties and jackets at all times, except Sunday lunchtimes.

Julie Fadden remembers it well: **"Allinson's was a real cabaret club with lamps on the tables. We once saw a magic act that went wrong and the woman couldn't get out of the trunk and they were having a dispute in the middle of the act. Hilarious!"**

Its most popular compere was Al Nolan. The venue formed one third of Liverpool's cabaret trio of The Shakespeare in the city centre and the Wooky Hollow in West Derby, and played host to acts including Bob Monkhouse, Tom O'Connor, Frankie Vaughan, Val Doonican, The Crickets, Del Shannon, Pete Price and Micky Finn.

Pete Price, now a Radio City DJ, says: "I ran The Shakespeare. One night Dorothy Squires was playing for us but left her bra at Allinson's. I had to drive all the way there to get it or she wouldn't go on."

Mark Cowley worked in the cabaret band as a youngster. He says: "Every night's entertainment would have a warm up act followed by a comedian like Jackie Hamilton, Micky Finn, Tom O'Connor and the late great Ray Kingsley (Arthur Smeathurst), or Norman Collier. The headline would be the likes of The Black Abbots (including Russ Abbot), Shine, Billy Elvis, Patti Boulaye, New Faces, Cannon and Ball, Freddie, with the cool resident backing band in the small stage attached to left of stage."

There was also a club on the same site, known initially as the Wispa, and later as Clouds and Secrets, where the door policy was more relaxed.

Colin Evans recalls an interesting night at the Wispa. "I still remember it now. It was probably about 1975, and I was 20. I can't remember what the actual night out was for, but they were pretty lenient at the Wispa about letting a crowd in.

"It was a Friday, and I went straight to work for

Saturday morning overtime. I got 'distracted' for a few hours after the club had closed, if you know what I mean."

Dulcie Green adds: "The Wispa was grab a granny on a Thursday, as was the Grafton."

Both venues closed in March 1983 after attendances fell. A new venue, Secrets, opened in 1990, but also closed. The site was demolished in 2003.

Micky Finn was one of many sad to see it go. He said at the time: "It felt like the London Palladium to me. I was quite keen to get hold of a brick and keep it as a memento of all those great times."

The Coconut Grove/Annabelles

A little bit of the Caribbean in Tuebrook, The Coconut Grove was the place to be, particularly on a Sunday night.

DJ Billy Butler remembers it well. "It was a fabulous place to be, back in the day," he says. "It used to be a cabaret club as well as a disco. They'd have some great acts on and they used to serve up your food in a coconut shell. We thought it was the height of sophistication."

One of the highlights was the amazing dance shows, put on by Norah Button, Liverpool's dance teacher to the stars, who later mentored comedian Les Dennis, Heidi Range from Sugababes, and actors Sam Kane and Graham Bickley.

In the '70s Miss Norah used to bring her girls to clubs around the city, including the Coconut Grove.

Natalie Young was one of the dancers. She says: "I started around 1976 or '77. We did the Hawaiian cabaret there. It was fantastic."

Friend Jools Foley remembers: "We worked with Norman Thomas, Peter Adamson and many others. We were the Tahitian dancers. Aloha!

"It was a haze of rushing from one gig to the next with false eyelashes and costumes all in the back of Miss Norah's car. There was one we did in Nottingham. Also The Millionaire Club? Or is that just what we called it?"

Tricia Liedl adds: "It was Kathy who set her grass skirt on fire with one of the candles we used for the candle dance. I remember some of the other clubs we worked at. We did Annabelle's, upstairs from the Coconut Grove, Mr. Pickwicks, Shorrock's Hill, The Cumberland Tavern, Gatsby's, and The Deerstalker and Chelsea Reach over the water.

"We were due to start at the Shakespeare club and a few of us turned up with Norah and Yvonne with all our costumes only to find it had burned down the night before."

Linda Davidson recalls: "We also did Christmas shows at the Centre Hotel. Shirley used to make share a room with her because I was only 15 - 15 and dancing in a bikini with bijous and feathers! We had the time of our lives!"

Sarah Waddleton was a regular at The Coconut Grove in the '70s. She says: "We used to love it! I remember being dropped off in my boyfriend at the time's Ford Capri, thinking I was very sophisticated. I had a pair of white stillettos and I used to wear them with big wide-legged trousers with a high waist.

"The palm trees may have been plastic, and the weather outside was blowing a gale, but to me it was like a tropical paradise."

The door policy was notoriously strict - with Bob Geldof and the Boomtown Rats being turned away for looking 'like scalliwags'. They returned, properly dressed, and were later allowed in.

Karen Burns Barnes almost didn't get into her own party: "I had my 18th birthday party at the Coconut Grove, but they didn't want to let me in because they didn't believe I was 18. I had a coach load of friends on the bus. I remember drinking blue lagoons and dancing all night."

Bernie Hunt remembers: "The Coconut Grove also has a seat fashioned as a boat to the left on the way in, and cloak room on the right. Also had a small flight of steps that the doormen loved throwing problem customers down."

Upstairs, Annabelle's was a doubles bar with a glass dance floor like Saturday Night Fever, with coloured lights underneath.

"I'd never seen anything like it in real life," says Sarah. "We thought we were Donna Pescow, but sadly my date looked nothing like John Travolta - and didn't dance much like him either!"

Eddie Cotton recalls: "It was the place to be on Sunday nights as all the young 'uns from Tuebrook, Norris Green, Old Swan, Breck Road and all points west used to pack the place out.

"The lit-up dancefloor was primarily used by the 'good dancers,' but there was also a huge 'ordinary' dancefloor for the likes of me who was too shy and hopeless at dancing.

"DJ Phil Kelly broke lots of records (not literally!) there, including Mellow Mellow Right On and Michael Jackson's Off the Wall album amongst many others.

"You had to have your wits about you if you managed to get past Big Fred on the door, but it was a fab atmosphere with great people and music."

And it wasn't just for the grown ups, as Paul Grant remembers "I played for an Under 11s side in Tuebrook called East Villa in the late '70s. The league had their end of year awards at 'The Cokey' and all of the waitress wore hula skirts and strategically placed coconut shells!"

The Coconut Grove closed and re-opened as the Venue, alongside the Carlton Cinema building next door.

The Wookey Hollow

This Belmont Road cabaret club was owned by

body-building champion and popular Liverpool night-club owner Terry Phillips. He first won Mr England 1960, followed by Mr Universe (which he won four times), Mr World and the European and World Championships.

At various times he owned the Wookey Hollow in Belmont Road, Tuebrook, Pickwick's, in London Road, the Falcon Crest in Formby and the Knowsley Country Club.

The club had begun life as the Belmont Road Picture House on January 17, 1914. The facade had a Tudor style feature centrally placed over the entrance. It had 780 seats.

Over the years it was leased to the Associated British Cinemas chain, then taken over by an independent operator, becoming the Lido Cinema on in 1938, before finally closing in 1959.

In 1960, a new facade was added and it re-opened as the Wookey Hollow, showing cabaret and some great bands. This was closed in 1982 when it was damaged by a fire. Repairs were carried out, and it re-opened as a club, again known as the Wookey Hollow. It operated into the early '90s, but has since closed again. The building has now been radically altered and sells kitchen appliances.

The Musical Box

West Derby Road has seen a lot of changes over the years, but Diane Cain and her family have been selling records at The Musical Box since 1947.

Still open to this day, and packed with rare vinyl and secondhand gems, it's a must visit for music fans.

Diane's uncle Jack opened the shop when he came out of the RAF after the war, and her mum Dorothy took over on 1951.

Diane and her son Tony now run the shop, and know their customers by name. Many have been coming in since the '70s.

"They come in and tell me their ailments," laughs Diane. "And I tell them mine. I make them a cup of coffee and we talk about music. Sometimes they buy something, but I think it's mostly for the chat.

"For a lot of people it's easier than going all the way into town. They can park for free outside and have a good rummage. We get people coming in for all sorts."

In the '70s Diane also worked in her family's other record shop in Old Swan, and her uncle Jack moved to another shop in Muirhead Avenue.

She ran the Old Swan shop from 1959 until 1979, and her son Tony was literally born into the family business when Diane gave birth in the room above the record store.

Tony now specialises in finding rare vinyl for customers, and has become quite the detective.

Diane likes pretty much every style of music, but has a special fondness for '70s Motown and disco.

"I loved the music coming out of America in that

era," she says. "The songwriting in Motown and disco is just something else. We've not seen anything like that since."

Tony is a fan of prog rock and heavy metal, but like his mum, he has pretty eclectic tastes.

The Musical Box has seen various formats for music over the years - from 78s arriving in packing cases straight off the boats from America, through the 45s, the 33s, the cassettes and the CDs. They haven't taken the leap into digital, and say that vinyl is much more popular than CDs.

"People love the vinyl," says Diane. "It's a lovely way to listen to music. They said that CDs were the future, but give me a vinyl record any day."

The Grafton and The Locarno

A grand old lady of Tuebrook, famous for her grab a granny nights and Beatles gigs, they don't get much more iconic than the Grafton, and her little sister The Locarno.

Built as the Grafton Ballroom and opened in 1924, it had a purpose-built sprung floor able to accommodate 1200 dancers. It was built next to the Locarno Ballroom, which is now known as the Liverpool Olympia, and opens occasionally for events.

Over the years The Grafton has seen gigs from Joe Loss, Victor Sylvester, Duke Ellington and The Beatles, and it became a byword for a certain type of night out, as was shown when Liverpool were playing a European Cup tie in Turkey and in response to a banner reading "Welcome to Hell" someone made a banner which read "You call this hell? You wanna try the Grafton on a Saturday night!"

But for every person who bemoans The Grafton, you'll find ten who remember it with a smile or, more probably, a laugh.

Paul Stevens says: "For me the best night for atmosphere was the Grafton. They'd let anyone in. It was a big ballroom that had a mixture of DJs and dance band/group. It was awesome. I'd guess there'd be about 500 in there.

"The girls would be a mixture of grab a granny and decent talent. All the women would be dancing. Meanwhile the fellas would line up around the perimeter like Indians circling the wagon train waiting to pick off their prey. Brilliant. Especially all the older Scouse fellas giving it loads of real boss posing trying to impress their prospective bit of strange with a mixture of twinkling feet and sparkling one-liners. Always a fabulous laugh just watching them. Always a fight or two, but there would be a searchlight on the offending parties at the first sign of trouble and the bouncers would pounce like tigers to break it up."

Mark Ainsworth adds: "I think the reputation began in the early '70s - when The Grafton became known as Liverpool's leading grab a granny venue.

"On Thursday nights, adolescent young men from

Life at Coconut Grove

The Locarno, now the Olympia

The Grafton Orchestra

Diane Cain and son Tony at the Musical Box

all over the city would head for the Grafton in the hope of forging a brief romantic encounter with one of the city's thirty-something divorcees. They were rarely unsuccessful."

Bernie Hunt had a big birthday at the Grafton. "I had my 21st there, in its private suite. I think it was called Finnegan's Cave at the time, in 1978. It was situated at the back, upstairs. We spent most of the night dissuading Grafton members from trying to bunk in for the buffet we had laid on."

Jack Foster also remembers The Grafton and The Locarno from his youth. "I went there when I was doing a summer job as it was mixed ages - anything from early twenties up to mid-fifties age group, and it was great.

"Coach parties used to bus customers in from all over the North West for the Saturday night events. It started off as an old-fashioned dance hall with big

band sounds. In more recent times it became your traditional cabaret nightclub.

"It wasn't all grab a granny either. Downstairs was the easy-going music to suit all ages and all tastes with live bands always on stage, and upstairs was a disco in the true sense of one and was great for those who preferred that type of music, or you could alternate between the two. It was great.

"It got a bit sadder over the years as clubbers habits changed and it got left behind."

Pat Upton takes exception to the idea that Thursday nights were grab a granny nights. "Every night the Grafton was open for business was affectionately known as grab a granny night, with Saturday obviously being the main one.

"It never bothered me what it was called and to be honest there were some very fit grannies out there that I'd happily have grabbed."

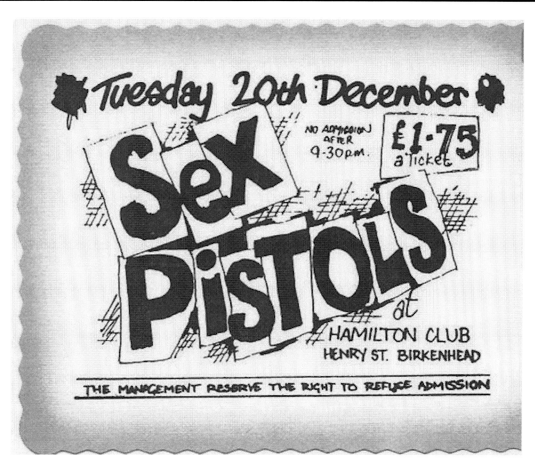

Chapter 11

Over the water: good times in New Brighton, Birkenhead and beyond...

After a difficult start to the '70s, Liverpool's nightlife scene was enjoying a resurgence. And across the water in the Wirral, there was plenty going on to entertain the Dirty Stop Outs.

Seaside towns like New Brighton were popular with crowds looking for a good night out, and the areas around Wallasey and Birkenhead had their fair share of pubs and clubs.

Debbie Jones was a regular in lots of New Brighton clubs, thanks to her mum, known to many as Twiggy. She says: "I must have left my shoes in every club in New Brighton!

"We must have been in them all - I never had to pay to get in any club because my mum, Twiggy, ran the top bar in the Golden Guinea for years - the famous people she met and the not so famous! Mum loved those days. We could go from club to club no trouble. The best was grab a granny night in The Tavern!

"She'd also worked in the Late Night Extra and The Creep. New Brighton had the best night clubs, they even came over from Liverpool.

"My dad was a doorman who worked with Rocky and Big Bob. My brothers worked all the doors.

"If you ask anyone in the club life, Twiggy was one of a kind. Everyone loved her and respected her - the life and soul of New Brighton."

Sue Hodrien was also a VIP in the Wirral clubs, thanks to her mum Norma. She says: "My mum worked on the taxis so I was well known in New Brighton as well as Seacombe.

"I saw Excess Baggage at the Empress. Loved the Golden Guinea, loved Twiggy, and all the clubs on the front.

"I loved the Late Extra and the Penny Farthing, The Grand and the Guinea. You could say I loved them all! The Creep under the fair was good, too. Twiggy worked there as well as the top bar in the Guinea. I got in all the clubs as was well known as Norma's daughter.

"Such lovely memories. But as I got older I slowed down."

Margie Owens adds: "My mum Betty worked in the

Greg Wilson
PROFESSIONAL DISC-JOCKEY AND PRESENTER

Denman Repro
Nottm. 4325

downstairs bar of the Late Extra Club and the Delmonte."

Clearly it paid to have a mum who worked in the clubs if you lived in Wirral.

The Chelsea Reach

"There was a bit of faded grandeur about New Brighton in the '70s," says Susan Mullin, who grew up in Elles- mere Port, but enjoyed lots of nights out in the seaside hotspot.

"The clubs there were good, you had a good crowd in, and if you were from our side of the water it meant you didn't have to brave the night bus through the tunnel - or spend a fortune on a taxi - on your way home."

Sharon Mason from Moreton agreed: "Other than for the big gigs at the stadium, or for a meal, we tended to stay on this side of the water, really. My favourite was the Chelsea Reach in New Brighton. We used to spend all day getting dolled up, doing our hair and make-up, then you'd walk down the prom and the winds would

be howling in and you'd end up looking like Worzel Gummidge. I've never known winds like it.

"We used to have a great time though, and because I was a nurse and worked shifts we'd often go there Monday nights, which were brilliant."

The Chelsea Reach opened in 1971, on the site of the Royal Ferry Hotel.

Terry Dobbins, also from the Wirral, was also a regu- lar on Monday nights.

"I remember getting kept in the club when the high tides happened - the car park at the side was on two levels. One night my Mark One Capri was at the top and my mate Steve's was on the next level down. Both cars were '70s customised with fur and tassels and lights - great at the time.

"We were on the balcony watching the tide getting higher and higher until the water flowed into his car.

"Thankfully mine was okay. But his face was a picture!

Jim Crabtree

Motown, Stax and Atlantic, with a smattering of Trojan Reggae for good measure.

"At 11 years old I began to spend all my spare money on vinyl, so by 1975 I already had a healthy collection.

"It was in this environment, spending countless hours sat behind the bar with my mum, bottle of Coke in hand, that I would have, at one point or another, got to hear most of the mobile DJs on this side of the River Mersey.

"Even when I went upstairs to bed I could still hear the muffled rhythmic thud coming through the floorboards and make out what tunes were being played.

"Often the DJs would leave their equipment at the end of the night still set up, to pick up the following day, and in the morning I'd sometimes seize the opportunity to have a look through their records and spin a few tunes, turning on the microphone and playing DJ."

On December 6, 1975, Greg made his debut as a club DJ at the Chelsea Reach.

"The Chelsea (as we called it) was somewhere [Greg's school friend] Derek and I had been managing to get into since we were 14 – we obviously looked older than we were, passing for 18.

"Back then nightclubs on Merseyside had a 2am license, with pubs having to close at 10.30pm. The Chelsea Reach was open until around 11.45pm."

The Chelsea was unusual in that it opened seven nights a week, and was usually full.

"When I was asked to fill in on that first Saturday night by the manager of the Chelsea, Bill Traynor, following a further mobile booking upstairs, it was an opportunity, although pretty daunting at the time, that I made the most of," Greg adds. "I'd be asked back the following week and would end up working there until 1978.

"The following month I was also approached to work at another local nightspot, the Penny Farthing Club, run by brothers Danny and Tommy Tsang, and by the time I left school I was DJ-ing most nights of the week as this had become my career and I was probably the youngest professional DJ in the country at this point in time."

Carole Sumbler also remembers it fondly: "I remember the Chelsea Reach on New Year - they had a piper to play in the New Year. Fab memories."

Ians Walters has slightly less fond recollections. "I remember the time I went to the Chelsea Reach. I was dying for the toilet but the queue was massive, so I saw an empty Coke can on the floor I started to p*** into the can.

"Next thing the police raided the place and I was arrested for possession of can of p***."

Pauline Jones was also less fond of the club. She recalls: "My husband only went to the Chelsea once and

"Other times the floor flooded and we danced in the water. When the club night ended we would all walk down the prom to the Grand Pub. They were great days."

Sue Wray from Wallasey says: "We were there almost every night when it first opened. The dance floor always included a huge pile of handbags for each group of girls.

"We used to sit on the bench seats by the disco. If anyone else sat in 'our' seats, we were really miffed. I remember there was a very sophisticated cocktail bar on the left as you went in. Then you went past the cash desk, where they served curry sometimes, and into the main bar and disco. There was another big room at the back.

"I had my 21st birthday there. One of the DJs asked me out, and I was so flattered."

Next door to the Chelsea Reach, a future star in the making was learning his craft. DJ Greg Wilson recalls getting his first taste of disco when his family lived in a pub on the seafront, The Criterion, right next door to the Chelsea Reach.

"I was 15 and still at school," says Greg, in his blog blog.gregwilson.co.uk.

"I'd 'inherited' my brother and sister's seven-inch singles. I was extremely fortunate that my older siblings were blessed with such good taste, as the majority of these records were by soul artists on labels like Tamla

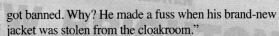

got banned. Why? He made a fuss when his brand-new jacket was stolen from the cloakroom."

Susan Mullin was probably one of the girls dancing to Greg's tunes on the dance floors of New Brighton.

"We thought we were like Pan's People," she laughs. "I used to go to Nesta Bellis Dancing School, and the girls from there used to meet up on a Saturday to go to the open-air bathing pool or walk up the prom, and we'd often end up in the Chelsea at night.

"One of my friends was spotted by a model scout and was in the final for Miss New Brighton. We all went to cheer her on. It was a big thing - Miss New Brighton used to get a place in the Miss England competition and then Miss World. She didn't win, but I think she got a modelling contract and a VIP membership to the Chelsea for it, and we all used to get in with her."

Susan remembers that girls used to get in to lots of clubs for free.

"I think it attracted the fellas in that way. You'd never have to buy a drink either, I think the men were a bit more gentlemanly. You'd never have to open a door or light your own cigarette when you were out."

The Golden Guinea

As the '70s drew on, Greg moved over to the Golden Guinea, where he worked from 1978 to 1980 as the resident DJ.

He says: "It was here that I really flourished, building my reputation not just locally, but throughout the Merseyside region, as a disco, funk and soul specialist. Apart from a short stint in Scandinavia, my life, throughout the late '70's, revolved around the Guinea, where, as I've previously put it, 'I became a big fish DJ in a small club pond'."

Phil Hough remembers the Golden Guinea fondly - particularly its happy hour.

"The Golden Guinea was a labyrinth of small rooms, three or four floors, some with bars, some without and a basement, great fun moving round in here.

"One Sunday night my older brother was over on holiday from Canada and me and my mates took him out on the lash, then to finish off at the Guinea.

"It was summer, a hot night and the style was denim and clogs. We were in one of the small rooms by the bar and I took the mickey out of my best mate so he poured his pint over my head. I just laughed and poured mine over his head.

"It was happy hour so we ordered another two pints and again my mate took a sip then poured his drink over my head again and I did the same. Everyone in there found this extremely amusing and started doing the same.

"My brother, who has got a few bob, was in hysterics so we doused him as well and he kept buying more and more beer and so it went on, soda syphons, fire extinguishers, the lot. The barman just kept pouring and pouring pints and just laughed along with us.

"We didn't get thrown out and even helped mop the mess up and we ended up on the dance floor like drowned rats."

Greg left New Brighton at the end of the '70s, making his name in Wigan and Manchester and becoming one of the most successful DJs of his generation.

"The new decade emphasised the need for fresh challenges," Greg adds, "and I finally left the Guinea and New Brighton for good, heading overseas once again for a few months, before getting my big break as resident at Wigan Pier, one of the most impressive clubs in the country."

David Roberts' band played the club three or four nights a week when it launched. He says: "I had the resident band in the Golden Guinea from its opening. It was quite a sophisticated place back in the day. I remember Twiggy who ran the upstairs bar. John Stanley was an old friend of mine from the '60s when he ran the Kraal Club, and my band the Pressmen were resident three or four nights a week. Later on I became a roulette croupier there until the Government clamped down on premises not licensed for gaming.

"New Brighton was full of great characters back then - Ted Gerry and John Brindle had the Late Extra. The Chase brothers ran the Chelsea. Jim Turner had the Travellers Rest and the Hotel Victoria. Great days. Great fun. I had bands in the Cabin Clubs of Liverpool and Birkenhead, the Porthole Cubs and may more. It was the heyday for nightlife. Just one long party."

The women really dressed up there, as Bridget Price recalls. "The Golden Guinea was quite smart when I used to go - we'd have been known to be in sequins and feather boas!"

Susan Jones adds: "I loved going out in the '70s in New Brighton. It has all the best clubs. The Golden Guinea, The Grand, The Chelsea, to name just three. Some good memories."

Christine Fogg worked at the Golden Guinea, as well as the Chelsea Reach. She says: "We used to go to The Late Extra, The Grand, The Penny Farthing, Grandma's and the Empress.

"I remember the Disco-Dine and Silver Slipper somewhere in New Brighton, but never went. Birkenhead was always the Cali and Liverpool was the Pyramid, Knightsbridge, Pez Espada occasionally The She and I am sure many, many others. A few large whites downstairs in the Slaughter House and who knew where the night would take you."

The Grand

Originally built in the 1850s, The Grand was relaunched in 1947 by film star Mae West. A 1953 advert for the hotel described it as "boldly situated on the broad seafront and commanding magnificent views of the ever-changing panorama of river and sea... a hotel of infinite charm, supreme comfort and personality".

By the '70s it was a popular nightclub, with a cocktail

lounge in the basement, called The Spanish Garden, serving tequila sunrises and blue lagoons, as well as the American bottled beer Shlitz.

June Mary Bell remembers it well. "My husband was the head doorman of The Grand when Jack Cook had it and I worked behind the bar. They were the good days."

Chrissie Josephs says: "I loved the Grand and the Chelsea - many a drunken weekend hugging the ladies loos!"

Jim Crabtree from Birkenhead was also earning his stripes as a DJ on the Wirral circuit at that point, playing the Chelsea Reach, the Penny Farthing and the Grand Hotel.

"I wanted to be a DJ for a few years so when I had saved up enough money, £369 I think, I bought a McGregor deck lights controller, speakers from Hammer Sound in Grange Mount, microphone from Radio Shack in Liscard," he says.

"A chance meeting at a fireman's strike fundraising event at the Grand Hotel New Brighton with the current DJ gave me a regular Friday night spot.

"They were great times, and such music. I remember playing Barry White Let The Music Play one minute and On The Trail of the Lonesome Pine from Laurel and Hardy the next! It was a crazy mix.

"My wife chose the current records and I chose the past ones.

"You got used to the crowds and knew what record would fill the dance floor with girls, boys or both.

"Wishing On A Star was the absolute end record for guys and girls to pair up."

There was a friendly rivalry between The Grand, The Chelsea Reach and The Penny Farthing. For Jim, also working the mobile disco circuit, it was a breath of fresh air.

"The atmosphere at the Grand was completely different from doing mobile club-to-club due to a number of factors - doormen would dictate the clientele who could get in, the cost, if any, of entrance, the DJ and music he played," he says.

"All of the time I was there not one single fight, I put that down to selecting music the club-goers that particular evening wanted to listen and dance to.

"I've got somewhere in the loft my appointment book with most of the dates times and venues of my mobile days. One 21st I did on Queen's Drive for a doctor's daughter who was calling almost every day with a list of records she wanted playing. During the Queen's Silver Jubilee weekend I played around three or four venues each day."

While Jim loved DJing, it was tiring work, particularly as he had a day job too.

"I worked in a wholesalers from 7.30am till 5pm, then I'd rush home for bath and tea, get dressed grab my two or three cases of records and taxi to the club.

"I'd finish around 2am then stay behind for drinks, get a taxi home, then a couple of hours sleep and do it all

over again, that was almost every night not just weekends.

"I'd meet my uncles at various pubs in New Brighton on Friday and Saturday just before I started work and on a Sunday I'd stay until last orders with them. I love history and they were all WW2 vets, so it was great to pry their history out of them one battle at a time. Other times we would go to the Apollo in Moreton. That was a hoot."

It was his day job which inspired the name for Jim's DJ business.

He says: "I worked at a cash and carry and I was looking for a name to call my disco, it was the rep from Phillip Morris Inc. who suggested Marlboro, so that's what I was called, even on my CB radio, I wrote to Phillip Morris chair, DV Littlejohn and gained his permission to use their logo, and had a lot of advertising stuff given to me - including a Red Marlboro jacket, a cigarette lighter, thousands of stickers. I even got to meet James Hunt."

The Penny Farthing
Jim was also a DJ at the Penny Farthing, just down the road.

"I still have some records and a letter from Buckingham Palace thanking me for offering my services at Prince Charles' wedding - that was done as a bet with Danny and Tommy Tsang, who owned the Penny Farthing club," he laughs.

"They were great guys and they bet me that I wouldn't write to Prince Charles offering my services at his wedding to Princess Diana - if I got a reply I would have free bar tab for a week."

Did they honour the deal?

"Not a chance," he laughs. "They were betting mad but so tight-fisted. Anyhow, my wife was one of the bar staff so it worked out good."

Debbie Jones adds: "Who could not forget the Penny Farthing? Danny and Tommy ran it - the funniest men I ever met. If you couldn't get in the other clubs you ended up in there. Because they knew my mum I got drinks for 50p. Those were the days."

Paula Slater also remembers the two brothers well. "My dad owned the Penny Farthing. He wasn't bothered about the rent, he was happy to have a few drinks on the house."

Mark Bennett also knew brothers. "Danny had a restaurant called the River View in Frodsham with Tommy.

"John Stanley had the Golden Guinea and I remember The Zoo under The Grand. John and Paul Chase had it then and the Chelsea.

"John lived next door to my girlfriend's at the time in Church Road, Neston.

"Rocky Hewitt, Stuey Jackson and Frank Lorraine were doorman then. Cliff Barnes was a doorman on The Grand as well.

"I remember The Bell in Waterloo Road - with its singles' night, Billy Blues, The Late Extra, The Empress on Vicky Road and The Creep, under the Palace.

"We used to do a pub crawl up Vicky Road - The Vicky hotel and Albion.

"Women used to put their handbags on the dance floor in the Chelsea and dance around them. You couldn't do that now - they would get pinched! Funny how things stick in your head."

"I remember the Berni Inn, where The Queen's is now on the front. A great steak house, and the caravan with cheeseburgers by the Penny Farthing.

"Some great nights. Now it's lost the glitz."

Rupert's

Wirral had enjoyed a thriving club and bar scene throughout the '60s, and in the mid to late '70s it saw another boom.

"My eldest sister saw The Beatles play at the Tower Ballroom quite a few times in the 60s," says Sarah Wilson (nee Morris) from New Brighton. "But by my time it was long gone. We used to go to Davey Jones' Locker, The Grand Hotel and The Empress, but I think Rupert's was my favourite - you always had to dress up and it felt like a proper night out."

Phil Hough was another regular. "Rupert's was a bit classier than most clubs on the Wirral, more difficult to get in although one of the bouncers and one of the owners used to play with us for a West Cheshire League football team so we always got in OK," he says.

"Pete Price and Vince Treacy were the DJs I can remember, and the scene was cool. One night I was very drunk and was in the basement disco and went to the toilet about five minutes before it was due to close.

"I fell asleep in the cubicle and eventually woke up about an hour later. When I opened the toilet door it was pitch black and I had to walk round the walls till I felt the bar, then round to the stairwell then luckily the door was still open - hands and knees up the stairs - and finally to the main entrance and reception where the last two bouncers were just putting their coats on to go home.

"The looks on their faces when drunken Phil on hands and knees looked up and said, 'Hello lads, what day is it?'"

Phil was a definite Dirty Stop Out back in the day.

"Other clubs I frequented on the Wirral were Grandma's, The Grand Hotel and The Empress in New Brighton, The Cabin in Birkenhead and The Waverley in Ellesmere Port," says Phil.

"We were out for fun, laughs the more the better.

"Many a time we would go across Argyle Street to the Dee Wan Chinese restaurant and continue the fun here. It had a large fish pond which one of my mates took a fancy to and he would quite often take a dip with the fish.

"He would always get thrown out but lots of patrons loved the commotion and on many occasions the regulars would say to us as we walked in, 'Is Willy coming in tonight?'"

The Tudor

Another popular bar was The Tudor in New Brighton, as Babs Gallimore remembers. "There was a club called the Tudor just on the opposite corner to Chelsea Reach. They had a big dance floor with square lights. Also Grandma's, a very popular club in New Brighton.

"The Grand was a really big club on prom too. I was a party animal in the '70s!

Susan Newlands also remembers the Tudor Club. "It had different-coloured lights under the glass squares making up the dance floor! Happy days."

The Gallery and The Empress

Wirral's rockers were well catered for at The Gallery, and on Friday nights at The Empress too.

Mike Coleman was working as a nurse at Clatterbridge Hospital, having moved over from Liverpool.

"I was a biker who, being particularly fond of rock music, bought a lifetime membership of The Gallery Music Club," he says. "My membership card was a metal military style dog-tag. The Gallery was popular with the female biker chick nurses from Clatterbridge Hospital, and they made up the most part of my companions when I went there.

"The Empress was more focused on the biker scene. The Wirral and Liverpool biker scene of the day still had an unhealthy obsession with historical feuds between bike-riding rockers and scooter-riding mods.

"For most of us bikers, our involvement was limited to paying lip service, the mimic of our dress code and occasionally acting tough while at the same time hoping to avoid any aggro.

"The scene made for a vibrant and mildly outrageous atmosphere at the aforementioned clubs. Although still working at Clatterbridge Hospital for a while thereafter I moved to a new home in Liverpool in August 1980. Visits to the Wirral clubs became less frequent and for me the biker scene became more centred around particular pubs rather than nightclubs.

"However as a rock music venue I was fond of The Moonstone in the St Johns shopping precinct and the legendary rock nights at the Southport Floral Hall, hosted by City Radio DJ Phil Easton (with his disco The Phil Easton Express) and frequent appearances by his friend Tommy Vance (a BBC radio show broadcaster who sometimes hosted Top Of The Pops).

"For reason of size and the number of people who went, the Floral Hall Rock Nights were by far the most vibrant, but on the negative side sometimes a little seedy with Miss Wet T-Shirt Contests and old '70s porn films projected onto a screen behind the stage."

Paul Martin from Birkenhead wasn't a rocker, but went to The Empress on other nights, and occasionally ventured into the bikers' big night.

"The Emp, as we knew her, was a nice old building," says Paul. "My brother was a bus driver and he used to go in the late '60s. The place was like a bus drivers' social. I don't know if that was an official thing or if they all just ended up there. He played in a band there for a while on a Saturday so we used to get in with him.

"When we got a bit older we started going on a Friday too, the famous rock nights. I was still at school but loved all the music and doing the stomp. I was a bit nervous of the bikers who drank Newcastle Brown Ale and wouldn't let us near their tables, never mind their bikes!"

Dunk Davis was a regular DJ at the Empress.

"I started in youth clubs at 14 years of age in Birkenhead, then mobile discos in the Empress Club in New Brighton," he says. "Then I went on to Davy Jones locker and The Craftsman's Club.

"I worked at Rupert's Club in Argyle Street, a great club, one of the VIP types, also the California Club

on Conway Street, The Golden Guinea and the Penny Farthing next door on New Brighton front. These were better than most in that area.

"My very first residency was the Compass Club in Grange Road East in Birkenhead. I loved working the venues. In the '80s I was a Radio City roadshow live DJ and again worked some great places, but the 1970s was the best time in my life. Everything was new and things changed every week - the charts, the music, fashion. People were so much nicer to one another, and you did slowies at the end of the night.

"I always played Just My Imagination by The Temptations for tap off time!

"The people, the music, the clubs - we'll never see the like again."

Perms, clogs and straightening your hair on the ironing board

Phil Hough and Jeanette

Phil Hough sent in these brilliant photos.

"The two big photos that are in black and white (yeah that old) are circa 1971. They were taken at our company apprentices' dance at The Boathouse, Parkgate," says Phil.

"Not a club as such but in those days Working Men's Clubs and dancehalls were the place to go around Merseyside. Showbands and mobile discos everywhere, then hit the Hamilton, Cabin, or Rupert's after.

Pubs and wine lodges were just for getting tanked up in before you went to the clubs as the drinks were too dear in clubs. Getting back early morning on the hourly tunnel bus and walking from Birkenhead home. God I must have been fit.

"A photographer was booked for the evening at the boathouse and the top photo is of us apprentices and our girlfriends, I am standing up far right. My girlfriend Jeanette - of three months - is standing next to

me in a blue halter neck top and maxi dress, so she tells me, as she is my wife now of 42 years.

"The bottom picture is more comfortable as I am back from the forced company photo to my mates. You can see the clobber we had on mainly Ben Sherman shirts, brushed velvet jackets and suits from Burton's.

"The two smaller photos, bottom one is again in 1971-ish and took in a Co-op hall in New Ferry. The top one was took a few years later when I got the quintessential footballer perm and am dressed all in denim with clogs on.

"When I finally got the bottle to have the perm done my hair was very long down my back and the barber said to me as he started cutting 'Did you go to Chegger Road School?' I said, 'Yeah how did you know that?' He replied: 'I have just found your school cap'.

"I frequented some great music venues and discos during the '70s such as The Cabin Club, Rupert's, Grandma's – Birkenhead, Quaintways and The Clockwork Orange – Chester and Reece's, The Mardi Gras, Victoriana, Drift Inn, Babalou, The Grafton and The She Club to name but a few in Liverpool.

"The tunnel bus was every hour from midnight till everyone had gone, jump on it and it was either singing or fighting or sleeping you took your chance. Many a

time I got a bottle of milk or orange off the milkman on my way down the A41 to my home."

Despite having to race for the tunnel bus, Phil was a regular at many Liverpool venues, as well as the Wirral ones.

"I loved them all and spent most Saturday mornings looking for clobber to buy and show off that night," he says. "For me, a mod, it had to be straight off a van from Carnaby Street and the very latest kit or I was not interested.

"Even on a few occasions going from New Ferry on two buses and the ferry boat to Flemmings in Walton Road to get made to measure jeans 24-inch parallels with gold (not white, that was for divvys) stitching.

"Put on your pair of ox blood cosmos shoes and a Ben Sherman and you will crack it with the girls that night."

His wife Jeanette also loved getting ready to go out.

She remembers: "Getting ready was a bit of a ritual taking several hours with instant tan and false eyelashes. I would sometimes use eyeliner draw 'Twiggy' lines under my eyes and along the eye socket.

"Hair was washed and rinsed with vinegar with egg white applied to make it thicker. It must have smelt very strange.

"We had no hair straighteners so we would lie with our hair on the ironing board and iron it through a piece of brown paper. The iron would come dangerously close to my scalp.

"I remember well some of the outfits I wore particularly a black handkerchief chiffon dress which I wore with pink platform sole sandals. I used shop in Miss Selfridge and Chelsea Girl.

"I wasn't really into the club scene. I did go to the Top Rank, Reeces, The She, Victoriana and Mardi Gras once or twice but preferred to go locally where I knew people and it was easier to get home.

"I can remember hitching a ride with friends to Quaintways in Chester to see David Ruffin. It was a lovely old building near the town hall with live music. I would only be 15/16 but everyone used to hitch lifts until they brought out films such as The Hitcher and we realised how dangerous it could be.

"If we went locally to the Lever Sports Club in Bromborough then the girls would often dance in a big circle with their handbags in the middle. I was very shy - having gone to an all girls' school - so I would drink Cherry B and Cider which helped me feel less anxious.

"Once you had a boyfriend you didn't go to clubs so much and we didn't seem to have girls nights out so much.

"My older sister Pauline once appeared on Top of the Pops as she was mad about the Walker Brothers. She used to get into a lot of scrapes trying to climb over walls to get in to see the stars wherever they were performing.

"My last memory of going to a club was when I went to my younger sisters 21st to a club in Argyle St Birkenhead. I was 32 and felt so old!! That would have been 1980s but clubbing was definitely for the younger ones!"

The Craftsman's

The Empress had a sister venue The Craftsman's in Birkenhead.

Paul Martin from Birkenhead remembers it well. "The owners of the Empress club in New Brighton were brothers, Jack and Billy McGhee. They had a club in Birkenhead, over Burtons in Grange Road, called the Craftsman's. The Craftsman's was a good night out, frequented by the same crowd from the Starboard Light or The Port Light Club by the old market. It had been the first night club in Birkenhead and it ended its days as the Cabin Club - one of those places where the drinks were cheap but you had to keep moving, or you stuck to the floor. The whole point of the place was you could continue drinking after 11pm. We thought it was amazing!"

Davy Jones' Locker

The central point of Egremont Promenade is the site of the Egremont Ferry, reached from Tobin Street. For a number of years there was a building there known locally as The Beehive. Before their demolition in 1983, there were also buildings which were part of a boat yard, the base for a motorboat club and also the infamous Davy Jones' Locker, which at various points was on a boat and in one of the buildings.

Phil Jones remembers it well. "It was in an old boat moored up against the sea wall, with a heavy wooden gangway to get on," he says. "It had an upstairs and a downstairs, quite small and got very packed in when busy. Health and safety would shut it down these days.

"It was a dump! I remember meeting a girl there, 1973, the day Red Rum won the Grand National. It was my mate's 21st birthday and we went to Aintree, won some money, got drunk and ended up in Davy Jones'. A day I'd rather forget as it turned out…"

Mike Wilson was another regular: "Don't think I ever went in there sober as we used to go there after the pubs had closed. Always got a stay-behind cos we knew the boss Ray Wood. I think there was some connection with the Melody Inn Club in Grove Road. I remember it always being freezing in the winter and hot in the summer cos the windows wouldn't open. Got a reputation for being a bit of a dive and was a bit scruffy but had good beer, good music and 'flexible' opening hours. What else could a bunch of young lads want?"

The Cap

The Capitol had been a thriving cinema, opening in 1926 with Midnight Sun staring Laura La Plante and Pat O'Malley. With 1,390 seats, it had a large balcony and an impressive tiered rake, which overlooked a full orchestra that offered musical entertainment before, during and after films.

Inside there were mahogany panels and fine plasterwork depicting three galleons in full sail. The front of the building was finished in glazed terracotta with a large verandah which shielded those queuing outside from the rain.

Unfortunately the fancy auditorium couldn't disguise poor acoustics, made worse when the 'talkies' came along. In 1959 the Capitol closed to undergo a complete modernisation programme - reopening two months later as ABC Cinema. Despite all the changes the ABC Cinema struggled to recover its popularity. Many of the patrons deciding to find alternative form of entertainment and in the early 1970s, the Capitol closed its doors, showing Cliff Richard's Take Me High as the last film, on February 23, 1974.

The building reopened as a bingo and club in 1978, hosting gigs and disco nights, and known as The Cap.

Mark Bennett says: "The Cap was where the ABC pictures were in Liscard. I knew the fella who owned it, George Armstrong. He had the bingo as well."

Julie Williamson describes it as "the best club ever, as I love rock music", adding: "They were playing

Genesis, Phil Collins and Thin Lizzy. The building is still there - it was above the ABC picture house.

"I then moved into the posh part and went to many a disco at Westwood Grange Country Club, which is now The Red Fox. When I went there in early '70s, it was just an old house you used to pay on door to get in to."

The Oasis

Another Wallasey rock venue was The Oasis on Park Road West.

Martin McMullin remembers heading there on Thursday nights in the early '70s.

"It was in the basement of one of the huge detached Victorian houses in Park Road West," he says. "We used to go there every week for the rock night. They had a resident band, who were very good.

"There were another couple of rock clubs which we used to go to after the Oasis. One was the Lamplight in Poulton Road Wallasey, and another was the Empress in New Brighton."

The Lamplight

Poulton club The Lamplight on Lindeth Avenue has fond memories for Sue Reay.

She says: "I used to go to the Cap in Liscard, the Embassy club Seacombe, Raker's club New Brighton and a little club in Poulton called The Lamplight, where I met my husband, in 1973.

"I was only 16, so shouldn't have been in the club, and my future husband was 21. He had seen me at a bus stop a few days earlier and then saw me in the Lamplight.

"He pinched my bum and then his friend pushed him at me to dance and the rest is history. That was in 1973 and we are still together.

"The Lamplight Club was above the garage owned by Ivor Motors on the corner. It was closed down because of the garage being below it. There was only the steps going up and no fire escape. I think it closed around 1975. We bought our first house in 1976 right behind the club and it was closed then.

"We were lucky on the Wirral, having so many choices - either Wallasey, Birkenhead or Liverpool. Great times and great memories."

Strawberry Alarm Clock

Janet Parrington used to go to this wholesome sounding youth club. She says: "I used to go to the Strawberry Alarm Clock. It was in a church hall attached to English Martyrs Church on St George's Road. You had to go and ask the priest for a membership card. It was on a Sunday night. Great times there."

Bridget Price adds: "I went there with friends from school. I remember dancing to I Heard it Through the Grapevine."

The Hamilton

Birkenhead cabaret club The Hamilton played host to

some of the bigger names of the day, including gigs from Motorhead and Slade. There was a planned Sex Pistols gig on December 20, 1977, but it was later cancelled and not re-booked.

Dunk Davis was also DJing at the Hamilton. He says: "The Hamilton was the best club of all clubs for me - seven nights a week. Great times. It was one of the best on Merseyside. The music I played was Motown and soul and USA funk bands. I was on all the mailing lists so got them before anyone else.

"I did a stint in Chester clubs but then came back and was at Mr Digbys club in Birkenhead, then, in 1974, the boss of the big cabaret and disco club the Hamilton offered me a resident job there as the DJ. I then went on to be the compere till 1979."

It was also where Terry Lennaine - of BBC Radio Merseyside's Keep On Truckin' Radio Show - used to play soul and funk records. His Monday night radio shows were hugely popular, and many music fans would head down to his get togethers at the Hamilton Club.

Greg Wilson was another regular at the club for the Get Togethers, as well as running his own nights at the Golden Guinea.

"The Hamilton was a cabaret club in Birkenhead, which would later become the Pleasuredrome," says Greg. "These were charity events held on a Wednesday, with the admission fee being a new toy, which went to children's homes. Terry was always a big supporter of homegrown black music, and I saw many classic, and not so classic, British Funk bands at these nights – Heatwave, Gonzalez, Olympic Runners, Hi-Tension, Delegation, Rokotto and the Real Thing included."

Leighton Court

Nights out didn't get much more fancy than Victorian mansion turned club Leighton Court, near Neston.

The house had been owned by William Jackson, a Liverpool solicitor. When he died, it became a casino, nightclub and disco.

Bridget Price says: "I remember Leighton Court. I thought I was the bee's knees if got taken there by a date in a sports car."

Sarah Wilson agrees. "As well as a disco, the club had three bars and a restaurant, and I remember the DJ was often Pete Price or Terry Lennaine."

Ceri Newton remembers: "It was very popular, coachloads came from all over. The light up disco floor downstairs was my favourite! I'm pretty sure the resident DJ was called Dave Wakeman, always played anything by the Human League. When I walked in as he said I looked like the blonde one from the band."

A fire badly damaged the building in 1988 and it was demolished.

Ralph Bulter (front, right) at the YMCA with Laurence Craven (third from left)

Chapter 12

Sun, sea and... Southport

A generation of pleasure seekers tripped the light fantastic at Tiffany's in Ainsdale, and stole a kiss on the River Caves boat ride at Pleasureland. Many travelled from Liverpool and Manchester to enjoy the sea air, and show off their dance moves at the Northern Soul half hour at the Dixieland on Monday nights.

The YMCA

Ralph Bulter says: "The YMCA in Houghton Street, Southport, was very much for the young teenagers. We used to play mainly disco and glam. The Somewhere Else was more underground rock and much more our thing."

Ralph sent in this great picture from the YMCA.

"Me and Laurence Craven used to do the disco and skating on a Friday and Saturday. I think it was a charity gig hence the girl speaking over our mic. This was probably around 1974. The Friday disco proved quite popular for the teenagers."

The Somewhere Else

"We also used to introduce bands at the Somewhere Else club in Neville Street, Southport on a Sunday night," says Ralph. "Apart from regular appearances from Strife there was an early spot for Judas Priest.

"With a long haired Rob Halford on vocals they were pretty terrible on the night. Norman, who ran the club, unplugged their gear and threw them out after two or three numbers, leaving us playing sounds all evening. They obviously improved, going on to great success."

The Dixieland and the Scoobie Doo

Debbie Taylor (nee Russell) grew up in Southport in the '70s and, together with her trusty group of school friends, had a great time in the town's nightspots.

"There were five or six of us girls who used to knock about together," she remembers, fondly. "We left school in 1976 and were affectionately known as 'The Class of 76'.

"A couple of pubs and bars that were around at that time were Toad Hall by the seafront in Ainsdale, The Sands, also in Ainsdale, The Midnight Lounge, which was by the Marine Lake in Southport, and The Scarisbrick Hotel, better known as 'The Brick' in central Southport.

"We used to go to Dixieland - better known as The Dixie - on Monday nights. My cousin was one of the bouncers on the door so used to get us in!

"The bar area was cordoned off but we managed to get a cheeky lager and black now and again.

"We sometimes went to the Northern Soul night - and tried to dance like proper Northern Soulers (Keep The Faith!) to Wigan's Ovation's Down Ski-ing in the Snow or Gary Lewis and the Playboys' My Heart's Symphony, or the heavy night on a Thursday. Deep Purple's Smoke on the Water is one I can remember.

"We also went to the Dixie sometimes on a Friday night, danced round our handbags. There was a mixture of music at that time, things like The Rubettes' Sugar Baby Love, Bay City Rollers' Shang a Lang.

"We all loved soul music, Archie Bell and the Drells' Soul City Walkin, Harold Melvin and the Bluenotes' Don't Leave Me This Way, Smokey Robinson's Tears of a Clown to name but a few.

"There were the disco numbers too, the Bee Gees' Stayin' Alive and Night Fever and Earth Wind & Fire's Boogie Wonderland."

Ken Nixon also remembers great nights at the Dixieland.

"I loved The Dixieland in the '70s. Friday nights were great - lots of nurses from Southport hospital - and sometimes on a Monday we'd go for the Northern Soul in the early '70s. We used to go on Saturday night and we used to sleep in the car in the car park, then on a Sunday we would go to the Scarisbrook Hotel for a 'livener' before heading home to Widnes.

"I was in Merchant Navy so I had a lot more spare time than my mates to get out and about."

Tom Abram was another regular at the Dixie. He recalls one night in particular. "The Dixieland with Bob Mason singing Ring of Fire. Met my wife there in 1973, when £5 was enough for a great night out."

Debbie and the girls also used to go to another venue round the back of the Dixie called the Scoobie Doo.

"This place wasn't licensed," she remembers. "It was really so young people - school kids mostly - could go and meet up and have a dance. The DJ's nickname was Happy. He was the brother of one of the lads in my class at school who used to get us tickets."

Tiffany's Ainsdale
On Sunday nights the Class of '76 would go to the famous Tiffany's in Ainsdale, now sadly demolished.

"The DJ was called Phil Whatten," she says. "He played a lot of disco music. Upstairs was a bar called The Bali Hi.

"It was hard to get in there, they were quite strict so we had to dress up to the nines. Bryan Ferry and Roxy Music were becoming popular so this meant dressing up like the Roxy girls - Jerry Hall - in pencil skirts, high heels and tights with a pencil line down the back.

"When we walked in to Tiffany's we felt like we owned the joint!"

The Dandy Club
The girls also used to call into The Dandy Club, on Neville Street, with its light up dance floor, just like in Saturday Night Fever.

"When I started work in 1977 I used to go there on a Thursday night straight from work with my friend," says Debbie. "It was ladies' night and they used to lay on a buffet. It was a cheap night.

"We would just buy a couple of cokes, eat their food and then dance."

Free food was a popular theme when we asked readers about their favourite Southport nights out.

Carol Bennion recalls: "We used to follow the free food buffets around. Monday, Toad Hall; Tuesday West End Club;, Wednesday was Shorrocks Hill; Thursday the Dandy Club and Friday the Sundowner - I don't think Minoo stretched to free food there, though. Saturday was Dixieland. Tiffany's was any night. Happy days and happy memories."

The Kingsway
Another key club in Southport at that point was the Kingsway, also known as Kingsway Club, and Bliss.

It was a nightclub and casino built in 1931 in an art deco style, with large portrait windows and hexagonal turrets with hexagonal windows, at the south end of Southport Promenade.

It was constructed over three floors, the basement being a bar, the ground floor being a nightclub, and the top floor being a casino.

On 22 January, 1962, the Beatles had their first gig at Kingsway, which was then known as the Kingsway Club. The following month, Ringo Starr made his debut with the Beatles there, when he replaced then-drummer Pete Best, who was ill at the time.

Later that decade Tom Jones, Larry Grayson, Tom O'Connor, Cilla Black and Engelbert Humperdinck also played the venue. Norman Wisdom called in while filming What's Good for the Goose at the Birkdale Palace Hotel in 1969.

Cabaret acts were booked for the week, and audiences were thin on the ground Monday to Thursday.

"Towards the end of the '70s I would occasionally go there," says Debbie.

"This was a casino but there were a couple of dance floors, one in particular called The Sundowner. I 'acquired' an ashtray from there - not that I smoked - and I still have it to this day."

It was also very popular during the 1980s punk era and the 1990s dance era. In the late '90s it was renamed Bliss. It also added a bingo hall.

The nightclub and bar closed in 2004 and reopened for a short time during 2006 before closing its doors for the last time in 2007. In 2008 plans were put

forward to demolish the site and build a luxury hotel, apartments and retail complex, none of which came to fruition. In 2010, a major fire destroyed the derelict building and it was demolished two days later.

The El Cabala Coffee House

This Eastbank Street coffee house was the place to be seen in Southport in the '60s, with the town's well-heeled intellectual ordering black coffees and French pastries and regularly making them last all day.

On the site taken over by the Gallery grill, it was open in the daytime and evenings.

By the '70s it was still seen as a cool option, and a number of readers wrote to us about the posh girls and lads who would meet there for exotic-sounding coffees at twice the price of anywhere else.

Debbie Taylor remembers it well. "This was supposed to be trendy and a place to be seen. Frothy coffee with chocolate on the top in big wide cups. Sounds daft now, but it was hard to get a seat."

Fashions - centre partings, henna, loons and cheese cloth

Debbie Taylor: "When we were at school most of us wore our hair long, parted down the middle. I eventually had mine cut short, it's still short today.

"Most of us used to colour our hair with those Hint of a Tint wash in, wash out products. I subsequently discovered henna and used that on a regular basis.

"My dad used to have a fit and said it smelt like s--- !

"Towards the end of the 70s I offered to model my hair for one of the hairdressing salons in Southport. I had a stack perm on one side of my head, straight on the other side. It was blonde on the top, dark brown underneath and it had three light brown streaks on top.

"When I went into work everyone thought I was some kind of punk! My mum and dad hated it. It took me a while to get used to it I can tell you but I did get noticed in the street.

"Clothes sort of varied throughout this era for me - loons and cheese cloth shirts, tank tops, baggy jeans.

"One friend and I went through a stage of buying exactly the same clothes but in different colours.

"For example she had a navy midi skirt, I had a brown one, she had a yellow short-sleeved jumper with cable pattern on it, mine was white. Then there was the sophisticated look (or so I thought!) pencil skirts etc.

"I used to make a lot of my clothes in those days because although I had Saturday jobs, I didn't have a great deal of money.

"Grandad shirts and drain pipe jeans were fashionable. I used to explore the secondhand shops for old men's shirts, cut the collars off and sleeves, they looked great.

"It was hard to get drain pipe jeans (or drainies as they were called). My friend and I managed to get them in the Army and Navy stores.

"No-one seemed to sell them then.

"Northern Soul night dress code was different. Long sun-ray pleated skirts, small tops and those old fashioned sandals your granny used to wear were all the rage.

"The lads used to wear parallel trousers to their ankles, flat lace up shoes, tank tops or tight fitting shirts.

"Sometimes you would see some of the real serious Northern Soul lads in Southport during the day. You could always tell because most of them used to wear long leather coats.

"They thought they looked cool, and to be truthful, they probably did then.

"Heavy night was different again. A lot of students used to go so it was jeans and T-shirts mainly. I wore a black velvet jacket and long thin scarf too. Really dressed down!

"Etam's was probably the best shop for clothes although occasionally my cousin would take one of my friends and I into Liverpool to the heady delights of Chelsea Girl.

"Smock tops, polo neck sweaters, miniskirts along with platform wedges were some of my favourites towards the end of the '70s.

"I liked denim too and as I used to work in a shop called Easywear when I first left school. They sold jeans and I used to get a discount!"

Southport Open Air swimming pool

In the '70s, Southport's open-air bathing lake was still open, and brave swimmers used to splash around in salt water. The lake was in the form of an oval, 330 feet in length and 212 in width and was surrounded by a grass border and gardens. At its peak there were up to 1000 swimmers and double that number of spectators, and regular beauty pageants were held there alongside some occasional gigs.

The architect for the lake was Robert MacLaren Love, who died in 1979. The purpose of the lake, opened in 1926, was to provide a large open-air sea bathing lake for mixed bathing. It was situated at in the Prince's Park and cost £60,000 at the time.

There was also a lido in Ainsdale.

Debbie Taylor and the Class of '76 enjoyed the pool, particularly in the long hot summer of '76, the hottest for more than 350 years - and probably for much longer.

"When we were at school in the summer holidays we used to go to the Southport Open Air swimming pool," she remembers.

"We all used to buy a contract pass that was cheaper than paying daily. We used to go practically every day. The weather seemed to be better in those days too because we all managed to get a great tan.

"I used to use coconut oil so I must have fried - not recommended now! On good days the pool was packed.

"We used to constantly walk around to see if we could spot any nice looking lads. We all loved it particularly when we got to know the life guards. You were really someone if you knew the life guards."

Silcock's

"We used to go to the fairground on a regular basis too," says Debbie. "Our favourite ride was either the waltzer or the speedway. Usually the speedway because it was run by Herbert Silcock Junior and all the girls fancied him.

"I went to junior school with Mark Silcock, his brother. The Silcock family are well-known in Southport. They were particularly well-known during the '70s too."

The Moulin Rouge

The Moulin Rouge in Ainsdale played host to some big gigs in its time, including sets from Pink Floyd.

David Harrison was the general manager of the Moulin Rouge Ballroom and Latin Room night club in the '70s. "The Moulin Rouge was a 1000 capacity ballroom, after being converted from the former Plaza Cinema in 1957," he says. "The premises were situated on the site of the now Toby Inn on Liverpool Road, Ainsdale. When the premises were sold to Mecca they were converted to Tiffany's and in the first year I was General Manager before moving on to Park Hall Leisure Centre at Charnock Richard.

"The Moulin Rouge was primarily a dance hall and ballroom with live bands and regular Saturday night dancing whilst the Latin Room was a night club and disco with licensed bar until 2am."

The venue had an exciting, and eclectic, range of entertainments on offer, as David explains. "Bathing competitions, fashion shows, exhibitions, dance competitions, wrestling, weddings and many other functions were staged in the ballroom.

"Saturday night was a must for a night of dancing to the resident band together with supporting groups. Revellers from all around the area (Liverpool/Crosby/ Formby/Preston/Ormskirk) attended and finished the evening off upstairs in the Latin Room. New Year's Eve tickets were always sold out by the end of November. Happy days."

Early ad for Southport's open air swimming pool

A BATHING LAKE

The author

Jade Wright was the Liverpool Echo's music writer for more than a decade, reviewing gigs and interviewing some of the biggest bands in the world. As part of that she wrote about Liverpool's entertainment scene past and present, as well as Scouse bands making their mark on the world.

Sadly too young to go to The Cavern or Eric's, she was fascinated by tales of Liverpool's cultural and social history, told through music, clubs and great nights out.

She now edits Good Taste Magazine - a food and lifestyle magazine - and also works as a freelance editor, writer and consultant, specialising in food, drink and entertainment for various publications.

Acknowledgements

Rikki Wright, without whom this book - or indeed my life - wouldn't have been possible.
My husband Marc Waddington and my daughter Beatrice.
Greg Wilson and his brilliant Being a DJ blog blog.gregwilson.co.uk
John Harrison and his Memories of Liverpool 8 Facebook group that provided pictures for the Timepiece, Ugly's and many others
Everyone who has contributed memories and pictures, and in particular Mark Thomas, Bill Leece, Ian Prowse, Phil and Jeanette Hough, Dave Wiggins, John Mcilwaine and Jim Crabtree. Thanks to Pete Hill for the pics.

The Dirty Stop Out's Guide trademark is owned by Neil Anderson.

Hofbrauhaus regulars